ES V

D1724092

Introduction

The Common Body of Knowledge

The Common Body of Knowledge (CBOK) study is an ongoing global research program funded by The Institute of Internal Auditors Research Foundation (IIARF) to broaden the understanding of how internal auditing is practiced throughout the world. The last edition of this study was conducted in the fall of 2006. The overall purpose of the CBOK project is to develop the most comprehensive database ever to capture a current view of the global state of the internal audit profession. The database contains information about compliance with The Institute of Internal Auditors' (IIA) *International Standards for the Professional Practice of Internal Auditing (Standards)*, the state of the internal audit activity (IAA), staffing, skills, competencies, and the emerging roles of the IAA. Some information was collected about the influences of cultural and legal factors about the development and practice of internal auditing around the world. The objective is to establish a baseline for comparison when the CBOK study is repeated in the future. The database will be updated to understand the evolution of global internal audit practices. Future studies will build upon this baseline, allowing for comparison, analysis, and trending.

Objectives of this Research Report

This research report includes all aspects covered by the CBOK questionnaires. Complementary to the global CBOK report, containing the worldwide findings, this research report focuses on the European results. More specifically, this research report provides the detailed comparative results for each of the 21 participating European countries. For each question, general results will be described as well as remarkable differences between countries allowing European internal auditors to benchmark themselves with their European peers. This research report is the first providing in depth comparative data on the status of the internal audit profession in Europe.

Types of Questionnaires

Three CBOK questionnaires were distributed:

(1) *Affiliates*. Numerous affiliates (chapters) work with The IIA headquarters around the world. This questionnaire also asked questions about how regulatory and cultural differences affect the application of The IIA Practice Standards. Please note that the results of this questionnaire will not be reported in this research report.

(2) *Chief audit executives (CAEs)*. Data on the status of the IAF within the organisation, application of The IIA Practice Standards, skills needed at each staff level and emerging issues were collected from CAEs worldwide.

(3) *General membership*. Data on how an audit is performed, skill sets needed and emerging issues were collected from internal auditors worldwide.

Who is Who?

Three research teams were involved.

(1) *Lead Team*. Priscilla Burnaby (Bentley College) – Project Coordinator and Team Coordinator, Mohammad Abdolmohammadi, (Bentley College), Susan Hass, (Simmons College) and Audrey A. Gramling, (Consulant) (Kennesaw State University) were responsible for North, Central and South America and the Caribbean.

(2) *Europe and Africa*. Rob Melville (Cass Business School, London) – Team Coordinator, Marco Allegrini and Giuseppe D'Onza (University of Pisa), Leen Paape (Neyenrode Business School), Gerrit Sarens (Université Catholique de Louvain), Houdini Fourie, Marinda Marais and Elmarie Sadler (University of South Africa).

(3) *Australia and Asia*. Barry J. Cooper, (Deakin University) – Team Coordinator and Philomena Leung (Deakin University).

This research report is written by five members of the European/African team.

Responding Countries in Europe

The last edition of CBOK (2006) is the first study that invited The IIA's entire worldwide membership to participate. The participation of members from 91 countries and 9,366 useable respondents makes this edition of CBOK the most comprehensive study in The IIA's history. More specifically, 2,773 useable responses were received from European members. This research report is based on these responses. The following table shows the response rate per country and the proportion of each country.

Country	Number of IIA Members (30 June 2006)	Number of Useable Responses	Response Rate at Country Level %	Proportion of Useable Responses %
Austria	277	97	35.0	3.5
Belgium	1,154	102	8.8	3.7
Bulgaria	357	90	25.2	3.2
Cyprus	276	29	10.5	1.0
Czech Republic	886	186	21.0	6.7
Estonia	135	15	11.1	0.5
Finland	584	43	7.4	1.6
France	2,937	281	9.6	10.1
Germany	1,728	157	9.1	5.7
Italy	2,531	495	19.6	17.9
Netherlands	1,741	113	6.5	4.1
Norway	662	45	6.8	1.6
Poland	520	98	18.8	3.5
Portugal	375	136	36.3	4.9
Romania	214	72	33.6	2.6
Spain	1,556	261	16.8	9.4
Sweden	542	68	12.5	2.5
Switzerland	305	33	10.8	1.2
Turkey	554	92	16.6	3.3
UK & Ireland	7,185	282	3.9	10.2
Totals	**24,975**	**2,773**	**11.1**	**100,0**

Table of Content

List of Tables

Executive Summary

1 Personal Background of Respondents

1.1 IIA Membership

60 % of the respondents became member of The IIA less than 5 years ago. About one third has been member for 6 years or more.

1.2 Highest Level of Education

One third of the respondents have a master degree in business, whereas 23 % has a bachelor degree in business. The proportion of respondents with a degree in other areas than business is smaller, respectively 13 % bachelors and 16 % masters.

1.3 Academic Majors

Economics, accounting, general management and finance seem to be the most popular academic majors of the respondents.

1.4 Position in the Organization

About 30 % of the respondents were Chief Audit Executives, whereas 22 % were Internal Audit Managers and 24 % Internal Audit Seniors.

1.5 Professional Qualifications

Internal auditing and public accounting are the most common professional qualifications.

1.6 Professional Experience

On average, respondents have 6.9 years of experience in engineering, 6.8 years in management and 6.6 years of experience in internal auditing.

1.7 Years as Chief Audit Executive

On average, CAEs have been in this position for 6.1 years, ranging from 0 to 44 years.

1.8 Reporting Status in the Organization

Overall, 36 % of the CAEs describe their internal audit function as being an independent position reporting to the audit committee, whereas 29 % describe their internal audit function as an officer position reporting to executive management.

2 Organizational Characteristics

2.1 Type of Organization

Listed and privately held companies make up for almost 60 % of the responding companies. Public sector and governmental organizations represent about one fourth of the respondents. Consultancy organizations as well as not-for-profit organizations are least represented. In general, almost half of the respondents are employed by international / multinational organizations, whereas 34 % is employed by a national organization.

2.2 Industry Classification

Overall, there is more or less an equal spread over all four industries. Financial service companies are best represented whereas manufacturing companies are least represented.

3 Internal Audit Function

3.1 Existence of an Internal Audit Function

The largest numbers of respondents work for IAFs that have been in existence for 0-5 years (34 %). Another 23 % of the respondents work for IAFs that have been in existence for 6 to 10 years. A small proportion of the respondents (16 %) work in IAFs that have been in existence for 25 or more years.

3.2 Corporate Governance and Internal Audit Documents

The corporate governance and internal audit documents that are most frequently used are

- Annual Internal Audit Plan / Rolling Audit Plan (82 %);
- Internal Audit Charter (70 %);
- Internal Audit Risk Assessment (67 %).

3.3 Appointment and Performance Evaluation of the CAE

In a majority of the cases (55 %), the Chief Audit Executive (CAE) is appointed by the Chief Executive Officer (CEO). In many cases (44 %), the chairperson of the Board is also involved in the appointment. The Chief Executive Officer's involvement is most prevalent also in the CAEs' evaluation (46 %) followed by the audit committee (39 %) and senior management (27 %).

3.4 Relationship with the Audit Committee

CAEs confirm that an audit / oversight committee exists in 60 % of the cases. On average, CAEs attended (entirely or in part) 4.3 meetings of the audit committee during last fiscal year. Of the responding CAEs with audit committees, 54 % regularly meet privately with the audit committee / oversight committee / chairperson. It has to be noted that for those responding companies with an audit committee, 88 % of the CAEs believe they have appropriate access to the audit committee.

3.5 Measurement of Added Value of the Internal Audit Function

The measures of "added value" with the highest overall average are:

- Recommendations accepted / implemented (48 %);
- Reliance by external auditors on the Internal Audit Function (31 %);
- Customer / auditee surveys from audited departments (29 %).

It has to be marked that 35 % of respondents state that their IAF does not formally measure the added value.

3.6 Internal Audit Planning

The majority of the responding CAEs (62 %) update their audit planning once a year, whereas 34 % update their audit planning multiple times a year. 84 % of the CAEs use a risk-based methodology to determine the audit plan, whereas 73 % takes into account requests from management.

3.7 Opinion on the Internal Audit Status

Overall, there is a general high agreement with the following statements:

- Objectivity is a key factor for your Internal Audit Function to add value;
- Independence is a key factor for your Internal Audit Function to add value;
- Your Internal Audit Function is an independent objective assurance and consulting activity;
- Your Internal Audit Function adds value.

4 Internal Audit Staffing

4.1 Number of Staff Members

Responding internal audit functions have, on average, 42 FTE (Full Time Equivalents). Staff members (juniors) represent the largest proportion, followed by contract audit staff (outsourcing or co-sourcing) and supervisors (seniors).

4.2 Incentives

The most indicated special incentives to hire internal audit professionals are Other (20 %); Transportation allowance (13 %); Relocation expenses (10 %); Vehicle provided by organization (10 %).

4.3 Vacancies and Missing Skill Sets

About one third (33 %) of the responding CAEs indicate that they had no vacancies at the time they completed the questionnaire (2006). The most common methods to make up for staff vacancies are:

- Reduce areas of coverage (29 %);
- Co-sourcing from internal audit service providers (25 %);
- Borrowing staff from other departments (14 %).

Only a small proportion of the responding CAEs (13 %) indicate that they had *no missing skills* sets at the time they completed the questionnaire (2006). The most common methods to compensate for missing skill sets are:

- Co-sourcing / outsourcing (49 %);
- Borrowing staff from other departments (20 %);
- Reduce areas of coverage (18 %)

4.4 Outsourcing and Co-Sourcing

The majority of the responding internal audit functions (73 %) currently outsource less than 10 % of their activities. The remaining 27 % currently outsource more than 10 % of their activities. More than half of the responding CAEs (56 %) expect that the proportion of outsourced / co-sourced internal audit activities will remain the same in the upcoming years. In contrast, 36 % expect the proportion of outsourced / co-sourced internal audit activities to increase in the upcoming years. The most frequently outsourced activities that are:

- Technical Competency Training for Auditors (24 %);
- Financial Auditing (23 %);
- Quality assessment of internal audit activity (15 %);
- Quality / ISO audits (10 %).

The most frequently co-sourced activities that are:

- Special Projects (10 %);
- Information Risk Assessment (9 %);
- Information Technology Department Assessment (9 %);
- Technical Competency Training for Auditors (8 %).

4.5 Staff Evaluation

73 % of the responding CAEs indicate that staff evaluation is periodically done by the supervisor. About 40 % indicate that auditee feedback is also used as a method of staff evaluation.

4.6 Training

On average, respondents received 132 hours of formal training over the last 36 months.

5   Internal Auditing Standards

5.1 Overall Use of IIA Standards

Overall, about 80 % of the respondents state to use (in whole or in part) the IIA Standards. In all 21 countries, the percentage of usage (in whole or in part) lies above 50 %. The most common reasons for not using the IIA Standards are:

- Management of the organization does not perceive compliance with the IIA Standards as adding value (16 %);
- Compliance with the IIA Standards is not supported by management (15 %);
- Compliance with the IIA Standards is too time consuming (13 %);
- Compliance with the IIA Standards is not appropriate for small organizations (12 %);
- Inadequate internal audit function staff to comply with the IIA Standards (11 %);
- Compliance with the IIA Standards superseded by local / government regulations or standards (11 %).

5.2 Adequacy and Compliance with IIA Standards

Most respondents believe that the guidance provided by the IIA Standards is adequate. The guidance provided by the Attribute Standards seems to be more adequate than the guidance provided by the Performance Standards. Overall, the Standards that are considered as most adequate are:

- AS 1100 Independence and Objectivity (92 %);
- AS 1200 Proficiency and Due Professional Care (90 %);
- AS 1000 Purpose, Authority and Responsibilities (90 %).

In contrast, Performance Standard 2600 (Management's Acceptance of Risks) and Attribute Standard 1300 (Quality Assurance and Improvement Program) are considered as the least adequate.

For all IIA Standards, the level of full compliance is lower than 70 %. Particularly, the IIA Standards with the highest degree of compliance are:

- AS 1100 Independence and Objectivity (67 %);
- PS 2400 Communicating Results (62 %);
- AS 1000 Purpose, Authority and Responsibilities (61 %);
- AS 1200 Proficiency and Due Professional Care (59 %).

5.3 Adequacy of Practice Advisories

The Practice Advisories that are considered as the most adequate are:

- PA 1100 Independency and Objectivity (87 %);
- PA 1000 Purpose, Authority and Responsibilities (87 %);
- PA 1200 Proficiency and due Professional Care (86 %).

5.4 Quality Assessment and Improvement Program

AS 1300 on Quality Assurance and Improvement Program (QAIP) has the lowest percentage of compliance: 29 % indicates that there are no plans to put in place a QAIP in the next twelve months; 27 % states that their organization currently has a QAIP; 22 % points out that a QAIP will be put in place within the next twelve months (at the time they completed the questionnaire). Only 23 % of the respondents indicate that their internal audit activities have been subject to an internal assessment within the last 12 months and an additional 7 % indicate that an assessment has taken place within the last five years. Besides, 42 % of the respondents state that their IA function have never had an internal assessment.

Only 14 % of the respondents indicate that their IA activities have been subject to an external review within the last 12 months. About 11 % has been subject to an external review within the last 5 years whereas 47 % have never had an external assessment. The most commons activities performed as part of the QAIP are:

- Engagement supervision (41 %);
- Use of checklists / manuals to provide assurance that proper audit processes are followed (38 %);
- Feedback of the audit customer at the end of an audit (36 %).

6 Internal Audit Activities

6.1 Internal Audit Activities

The four most common internal audit activities are:

- Operational audits (80 %)
- Internal control testing and systems evaluation (78 %)
- Control framework monitoring and development (62 %)
- Investigations of fraud and irregularities (61 %)

6.2 Evolution of Internal Audit Activities

When studying the overall evolutions in the period 2003-2009, results shows an increase in the importance of consulting / advisory, governance audits, information technology audits and management audits. On the contrary, we notice a decrease in the importance of compliance audits, financial process audits and operational audits. The proportion of fraud investigations remains stable over this 6 years period.

6.3 Resolving Major Differences around Audit Issues

In general, major differences around audit issues are usually revolved during the fieldwork and audit reporting, but rarely during planning and after the audit report is issued.

6.4 Reporting and Follow-up of Audit Results

In a majority of the cases, the CAE is primarily responsible for reporting audit results to senior management. In almost half of the cases (47 %), the primary responsibility for monitoring corrective action lies with both the internal auditor and the auditee, whereas in 35 % of the cases, this responsibility only lies with the internal auditor.

7 Tools, Skills and Competencies

7.1 Internal Audit Tools

The following audit tools are currently most extensively used:

- Other electronic communication (e. g., Internet, email);
- Risk based audit planning;
- Electronic work papers;
- Analytical review.

The tools that are currently less extensively used are:

- Total quality management techniques
- The IIA's Quality Assessment Review tools
- Process modeling software
- Balanced scorecard or similar framework

It is worth mentioning that for all audit tools, there is an expected increase in the use in the next three years.

7.2 Behavioural Skills

The most important behavioural skills for internal audit practitioners, regardless of their hierarchical position, are:

- Confidentiality;
- Interpersonal skills;
- Leadership;
- Objectivity;
- Team player;
- Work well with all level of management.

7.3 Technical Skills

The most important technical skills for internal audit practitioners, regardless of their hierarchical position, are:

- Forensic skills / fraud awareness.
- Interviewing;
- Negotiating;
- Risk analysis;
- Understanding business;

7.4 Competences

The most important competences for CAEs are:

- Ability to promote the IAF within the organization (80 %);
- Analytical;
- Communication;
- Conflict resolution;
- Critical thinking;
- Organization skills;
- Problem identification and solution;
- Keeping up to date with professional changes in opinions, standards and regulations;

7.5 Knowledge Areas

The most important knowledge areas are:

- Auditing;
- Internal auditing standards;
- Ethics;
- Enterprise risk management;
- Technical knowledge for your industry;
- Governance;
- Information technology.

8 Emerging Issues

8.1 Evolution in the Status of the Internal Audit Function

An IAF is mandatory in 64 % of the cases. Some 14 % expect this to happen in the next 3 years. IAFs are only in 24 % of the cases involved in strategy development. In 95 % of the cases, control frameworks will be implemented within the next 3 years. Training to audit committee members and organizational personnel is strongly on the rise. Providing assurance rather than consulting still remains the core business.

8.2 Changes in the Role of the Internal Audit Function

Respondents were asked to state if they expect an increase or a decrease for the following roles: risk management, governance, regulatory compliance, reviewing financial processes, and operational auditing. All five areas are on the rise in the next three years with risk management in the lead with over 81 % of the respondents expecting an increase, and governance on the second place with 64 % expecting an increase. The largest decrease is expected in the area of reviewing financial processes (20 %). IAFs are most likely to have also a role in the next 3 years in the following areas:

- Knowledge management system development (41 %);
- Strategic Frameworks (37 %);
- Alignment of strategy and performance measurement (36 %);
- Benchmarking (35 %);
- Corporate Social Responsibility (35 %);
- Developing training and education to organization personnel (35 %).

1 Personal Background of Respondents

In the first section of the questionnaire, the respondents were asked to complete questions about their personal background. More specifically, all respondents were asked to indicate how long they have been a member of The IIA, their highest level of education, their academic major(s), their position within the organization, their professional qualifications and their professional experience. Besides, CAEs were asked whether they think there is a need for additional certification beyond CIA for audit managers and CAEs, the number of years as CAE and their reporting status in the organization.

1.1. IIA Membership

Table 1 shows that 60% of the respondents became member of The IIA less than 5 years ago. About one third has been member for 6 years or more.

Table 1: How long have you been a Member of The IIA (%)

Country	Total Number of Respondents	1 – 5 years	6 – 10 years	11 years or more	I am not member	Total
Austria	92	30.4	27.2	33.7	8.7	100.0
Belgium	101	68.3	19.8	11.9	0.0	100.0
Bulgaria	73	94.5	1.4	4.1	0.0	100.0
Cyprus	29	72.4	27.6	0.0	0.0	100.0
Czech Republic	172	71.5	19.8	5.2	3.5	100.0
Estonia	15	73.3	26.7	0.0	0.0	100.0
Finland	42	50.0	26.2	23.8	0.0	100.0
France	271	71.6	11.4	4.4	12.5	100.0
Germany	144	54.2	22.2	11.1	12.5	100.0
Greece	76	73.7	26.3	0.0	0.0	100.0
Italy	464	73.9	18.9	6.7	0.6	100.0
Netherlands	112	63.4	21.4	14.3	0.9	100.0
Norway	45	40.0	40.0	20.0	0.0	100.0
Poland	86	2.3	74.4	0.0	23.3	100.0
Portugal	129	41.1	10.9	10.1	38.0	100.0
Romania	44	95.5	0.0	0.0	4.5	100.0
Spain	255	59.6	26.3	9.8	4.3	100.0
Sweden	67	56.7	28.4	14.9	0.0	100.0
Switzerland	33	27.3	39.4	33.3	0.0	100.0
Turkey	86	75.6	10.5	5.8	8.1	100.0
UK & Ireland	279	41.2	32.6	22.9	3.2	100.0
Overall Average	**2,615**	**60.3**	**22.6**	**10.6**	**6.4**	**100.0**

When comparing all 21 countries, we notice

- a high percentage of **new IIA members** (< 5 years) in Bulgaria, Cyprus, Czech Republic, Estonia, France, Greece, Italy, Romania and Turkey;
- a high percentage of **long term IIA members** (11 years or more) in Austria, Finland, Norway, Switzerland and UK & Ireland;

Note also the high percentage of non-IIA members in Poland and Portugal.

1.2.   Highest Level of Education

Overall, one third of the respondents have a master degree in business, whereas 23% has a bachelor degree in business (cf. table 2). The proportion of respondents with a degree in other areas than business is smaller, respectively 13% bachelors and 16% masters.

When comparing between countries, we see:

- a high percentage of **bachelor degrees in business** in Italy, Spain, Sweden and Switzerland;
- a high percentage of **bachelor degrees in other areas than business** in Estonia, Portugal and Turkey;
- a high percentage of **master degrees in business** in Belgium, Bulgaria, Czech Republic, Finland, France, Germany, Greece, Netherlands, Norway and Poland;
- a high percentage of **master degrees in other areas than business** in Belgium, Bulgaria, Estonia, France, Poland and Romania.

Table 2: Highest Level of Formal Education (%)

Country	Total Number of Respondents	Secondary	Bachelor in Business	Bachelor other than Business	Master in Business	Master other than Business	Doctoral Degree	Other	Total
Austria	94	23.4	8.5	2.1	38.1	3.2	12.8	11.7	100.0
Belgium	101	0.0	8.9	4.0	57.4	26.7	2.0	1.0	100.0
Bulgaria	71	0.0	2.8	1.4	52.1	42.3	1.4	0.0	100.0
Cyprus	28	7.1	21.4	10.7	35.7	10.7	0.0	14.3	100.0
Czech Republic	170	4.1	2.9	1.8	52.4	22.4	4.1	12.4	100.0
Estonia	15	0.0	20.0	26.7	26.7	26.7	0.0	0.0	100.0
Finland	43	11.6	11.6	0.0	55.8	18.6	2.3	0.0	100.0
France	268	2.6	7.5	5.2	51.5	27.6	3.4	2.2	100.0
Germany	146	7.5	29.5	3.4	45.2	8.2	5.5	0.7	100.0
Greece	76	0.0	26.3	5.3	42.1	18.4	6.6	1.3	100.0
Italy	460	20.4	42.4	17.8	13.9	3.7	0.7	1.1	100.0
Netherlands	113	0.9	5.3	4.4	55.8	20.4	8.8	4.4	100.0
Norway	45	4.4	13.3	6.7	57.8	13.3	0.0	4.4	100.0
Poland	87	0.0	0.0	0.0	57.5	39.1	1.1	2.3	100.0
Portugal	128	3.9	21.1	31.3	25.8	15.6	0.0	2.3	100.0
Romania	41	2.4	24.4	17.1	22.0	34.1	0.0	0.0	100.0
Spain	257	1.6	40.5	19.5	27.6	7.4	2.7	0.8	100.0
Sweden	67	4.5	46.3	13.4	17.9	9.0	1.5	7.5	100.0
Switzerland	33	9.1	45.5	6.1	21.2	6.1	6.1	6.1	100.0
Turkey	87	0.0	27.6	39.1	13.8	18.4	1.1	0.0	100.0
UK & Ireland	281	22.4	19.9	20.3	19.6	13.2	1.4	3.2	100.0
Overall Average	**2,611**	**8.8**	**22.8**	**12.6**	**34.3**	**15.6**	**2.8**	**3.1**	**100.0**

1.3.   Academic Majors

Overall, economics, accounting, general management and finance seem to be the most popular academic majors of the respondents (cf. Table 3).

When comparing the 21 countries, we notice:

- a high percentage of respondents with an **accounting** major in Belgium, Cyprus, Finland, France, Norway, Poland, Portugal, Spain, Sweden and Switzerland;
- a high percentage of respondents with an **auditing** major in Cyprus, Netherlands, Norway, Portugal and Spain;
- a high percentage of respondents with a **computer science** major in Finland, France, Poland, Switzerland;
- a high percentage of respondents with an **economics** major in Belgium, Czech Republic, Estonia, Poland, Spain and Turkey;
- a high percentage of respondents with an **engineering** major in Belgium and Czech Republic;
- a high percentage of respondents with a **finance** major in Belgium, Cyprus, France, Greece, Norway, Poland, Spain, Switzerland and Turkey;
- a high percentage of respondents with a **general business / management** major in Estonia, France, Norway, Poland and Sweden;
- a high percentage of respondents with an **information systems** major in Belgium, Netherlands and Poland;
- a high percentage of respondents with an **internal auditing** major in Belgium, Cyprus, Netherlands, Norway and Portugal;
- a high percentage of respondents with a **law** major in France and Poland;
- a high percentage of respondents with a **mathematics / statistics** major in Belgium, France, Poland and Switzerland;
- a high percentage of respondents with a **science / technical field** major in Czech Republic, France, Poland.

Note the high percentage of 'no specific academic major' in Austria, Switzerland and UK & Ireland.

Table 3:   Academic Majors (%)

Country	Total Number of Respondents	Accounting	Arts and Humanities	Auditing	Computer Science	Economics	Engineering	Finance	General Business / Management	Information Systems	Internal Auditing	Law	Mathematics / Statistics	Science / Technical Field	Other	No Degree
Austria	96	32.3	1.0	13.5	8.3	9.4	1.0	14.6	36.5	9.4	16.7	8.3	3.1	3.1	15.6	24.0
Belgium	101	44.6	7.9	22.8	9.9	50.5	12.9	39.6	30.7	15.8	26.7	15.8	16.8	8.9	10.9	0.0
Bulgaria	83	37.3	2.4	10.8	1.2	30.1	2.4	21.7	13.3	0.0	3.6	0.0	2.4	0.0	6.0	0.0
Cyprus	29	79.3	0.0	48.3	0.0	27.6	0.0	44.8	27.6	10.3	34.5	0.0	10.3	0.0	6.9	3.4
Czech Republic	186	19.9	1.1	7.0	9.1	54.8	12.4	24.2	15.1	7.0	11.8	7.0	8.1	10.8	5.4	1.6
Estonia	15	20.0	6.7	6.7	0.0	46.7	6.7	20.0	46.7	6.7	6.7	13.3	6.7	0.0	0.0	0.0
Finland	43	60.5	4.7	9.3	11.6	27.9	4.7	25.6	18.6	7.0	4.7	18.6	11.6	2.3	16.3	4.7
France	281	45.9	6.0	26.3	13.2	39.5	8.9	45.9	48.8	13.9	21.0	28.6	17.1	12.5	6.4	0.4
Germany	157	34.4	3.2	24.2	9.6	22.3	7.6	19.1	36.3	7.0	8.3	10.2	4.5	2.5	22.9	6.4
Greece	78	39.7	0.0	12.8	3.8	37.2	10.3	39.7	28.2	5.1	23.1	3.8	10.3	1.3	2.6	0.0
Italy	495	9.1	2.6	4.0	1.2	42.6	5.9	7.1	14.1	0.8	3.0	8.1	3.2	1.6	3.6	4.0
Netherlands	113	33.6	3.5	61.9	6.2	41.6	1.8	22.1	28.3	22.1	29.2	7.1	2.7	2.7	8.0	0.9
Norway	45	44.4	4.4	33.3	0.0	37.8	0.0	35.6	46.7	13.3	31.1	8.9	4.4	0.0	4.4	2.2
Poland	95	46.3	5.3	2.1	10.5	62.1	11.6	53.7	47.4	15.8	8.4	36.8	33.7	15.8	11.6	0.0
Portugal	136	45.6	1.5	40.4	4.4	25.0	5.1	23.5	33.1	11.8	25.7	4.4	4.4	0.0	2.9	2.2
Romania	72	20.8	0.0	4.2	5.6	30.6	8.3	22.2	12.5	4.2	13.9	11.1	5.6	2.8	4.2	0.0
Spain	261	42.9	1.1	31.8	0.4	47.9	2.7	35.2	36.0	5.0	18.4	6.1	5.0	2.3	5.0	1.1
Sweden	68	44.1	4.4	20.6	1.5	39.7	4.4	14.7	39.7	10.3	7.4	10.3	8.8	1.5	11.8	2.9
Switzerland	33	57.6	0.0	15.2	15.2	30.3	3.0	36.4	36.4	12.1	21.2	15.2	15.2	0.0	15.2	12.1
Turkey	89	38.2	1.1	25.8	2.2	62.9	4.5	42.7	33.7	2.2	19.1	16.9	9.0	0.0	3.4	2.2
UK & Ireland	282	22.7	10.6	9.2	4.3	16.3	4.3	10.3	20.6	10.6	16.7	7.4	7.1	5.7	7.4	18.8
Overall Average	2,758	32.4	3.7	18.7	5.4	37.8	6.1	25.0	28.5	8.1	14.9	11.3	8.1	4.5	7.4	4.7

Note that percentages do not add up to 100% as respondents could mark all that apply.

1.4.   Position in the Organization

According to Table 4, CAEs represent the largest group of respondents (almost 30%), followed by Internal Audit Seniors (24 %) and Internal Audit Managers (22 %).

Table 4: Position in the Organization (%)

Country	Total Number of Respondents	CAE	Internal Audit Manager	Internal Audit Senior	Internal Audit Staff	Other	Total
Austria	92	63.0	6.5	15.2	13.0	2.2	100.0
Belgium	101	20.8	29.7	21.8	22.8	5.0	100.0
Bulgaria	71	38.0	8.5	11.3	25.4	16.9	100.0
Cyprus	28	21.4	32.1	25.0	14.3	7.1	100.0
Czech Republic	170	37.1	12.4	24.7	23.5	2.4	100.0
Estonia	15	40.0	13.3	26.7	20.0	0.0	100.0
Finland	43	32.6	18.6	23.3	16.3	9.3	100.0
France	270	29.6	19.6	23.7	23.7	3.3	100.0
Germany	146	29.5	23.3	25.3	13.0	8.9	100.0
Greece	76	21.1	30.3	26.3	14.5	7.9	100.0
Italy	462	28.6	21.4	17.1	25.8	7.1	100.0
Netherlands	113	23.9	26.5	26.5	15.0	8.0	100.0
Norway	45	26.7	24.4	17.8	15.6	15.6	100.0
Poland	87	9.2	23.0	54.0	12.6	1.1	100.0
Portugal	128	13.3	22.7	21.9	32.8	9.4	100.0
Romania	41	9.8	14.6	26.8	36.6	12.2	100.0
Spain	256	37.9	27.7	22.3	9.0	3.1	100.0
Sweden	67	31.3	11.9	20.9	29.9	6.0	100.0
Switzerland	33	45.5	15.2	30.3	6.1	3.0	100.0
Turkey	87	36.8	14.9	28.7	11.5	8.0	100.0
UK & Ireland	281	25.6	28.1	29.2	13.2	3.9	100.0
Overall Average	**2,612**	**29.5**	**21.6**	**23.7**	**19.3**	**5.9**	**100.0**

1.5.   Professional Qualifications

Table 5 shows that internal auditing and public accounting are the most common professional qualifications.

When comparing all 21 countries, we notice

- a high percentage of **internal auditing** qualifications in Belgium, Estonia, Germany, Greece, Netherlands, Norway and UK & Ireland;
- a high percentage of **information systems auditing** qualifications in Netherlands, Norway, Sweden and UK & Ireland;
- a high percentage of **government auditing** qualifications in Bulgaria, Czech Republic, Norway, Poland and Sweden;
- a high percentage of **control self-assessment** qualifications in Belgium and Italy;
- a high percentage of **public accounting** qualifications in Cyprus, Netherlands, Switzerland and Turkey;
- a high percentage of **management accounting** qualifications in France, Sweden and Switzerland;
- a high percentage of **accounting (technician)** qualifications in Cyprus and Portugal;
- a high percentage of **fraud examination** qualifications in Belgium, Cyprus and Turkey;
- a high percentage of **financial services auditing** qualifications in Estonia, Finland and Romania;
- a high percentage of **fellowship** qualifications in Cyprus, Spain and UK & Ireland;
- a high percentage of **certified financial analyst** qualifications in Estonia, Norway, Romania and Switzerland.
- a high percentage of **other** qualifications in Austria, Bulgaria, Poland and Switzerland.

Furthermore, Table 6 shows that 65% of the responding CAEs agree that there is a need for additional certification beyond CIA for *audit managers*. When comparing all 21 countries, we see a high percentage of CAEs indicating a need for additional certification for *audit managers* in Cyprus, Finland, France, Norway and Spain.

Besides, 63% of the responding CAEs agree that there is a need for additional certification beyond CIA for *CAEs*. A comparison between all 21 countries reveals a high percentage of CAEs indicating a need for additional certification for *CAEs* in Finland, France and Spain.

Table 5: Professional Qualifications (%)

Country	Total Number of Respondents	Internal Auditing	Information Systems Auditing	Government Auditing	Control Self-Assessment	Public Accounting	Management / General Accounting	Accounting – Technician Level	Fraud Examination	Financial Services Auditing	Fellowship	Certified Financial Analyst	Other
Austria	96	20.8	7.3	1.0	1.0	3.1	2.1	6.3	2.1	1.0	1.0	1.0	37.5
Belgium	102	55.9	9.8	0.0	8.8	10.8	2.9	2.0	8.8	2.9	1.0	1.0	12.7
Bulgaria	87	6.9	0.0	8.0	1.1	4.6	6.9	1.1	4.6	0.0	0.0	0.0	31.0
Cyprus	29	44.8	3.4	3.4	6.9	58.6	0.0	13.8	13.8	0.0	24.1	0.0	0.0
Czech Republic	186	39.8	4.8	13.4	0.5	10.2	6.5	0.5	3.8	2.7	0.5	0.0	18.8
Estonia	15	46.7	6.7	6.7	6.7	6.7	6.7	6.7	0.0	6.7	0.0	6.7	26.7
Finland	43	41.9	9.3	4.7	4.7	7.0	0.0	0.0	0.0	4.7	0.0	0.0	25.6
France	281	24.2	5.7	2.5	3.2	14.2	13.5	1.8	2.1	3.9	0.4	0.4	23.1
Germany	157	65.0	9.6	0.0	4.5	4.5	1.9	0.0	2.5	0.6	5.1	0.0	21.7
Greece	78	51.3	9.0	0.0	7.7	9.0	1.3	0.0	5.1	0.0	0.0	1.3	16.7
Italy	495	29.1	3.8	2.0	11.3	11.7	0.6	4.2	1.8	1.6	0.6	0.4	20.6
Netherlands	113	47.8	20.4	4.4	2.7	47.8	2.7	1.8	0.9	0.0	0.0	0.0	23.9
Norway	45	46.7	15.6	8.9	6.7	22.2	8.9	2.2	0.0	0.0	0.0	2.2	28.9
Poland	96	28.1	2.1	8.3	2.1	7.3	3.1	8.3	0.0	1.0	0.0	0.0	40.6
Portugal	136	32.4	4.4	2.9	2.2	7.4	5.1	32.4	2.2	1.5	0.0	0.7	15.4
Romania	72	15.3	1.4	6.9	4.2	8.3	8.3	1.4	4.2	5.6	0.0	2.8	22.2
Spain	261	24.5	3.8	0.4	1.1	6.1	6.1	2.3	1.1	1.1	7.7	1.5	20.3
Sweden	68	17.6	19.1	8.8	4.4	14.7	16.2	1.5	1.5	2.9	1.5	0.0	20.6
Switzerland	33	42.4	12.1	3.0	6.1	39.4	15.2	6.1	0.0	3.0	0.0	3.0	33.3
Turkey	90	33.3	4.4	3.3	1.1	31.1	5.6	4.4	11.1	2.2	1.1	0.0	12.2
UK & Ireland	282	60.3	14.2	7.4	1.1	18.1	6.0	8.5	1.8	0.4	7.4	0.4	16.7
Overall Average	2,765	36.0	7.2	4.1	4.4	13.6	5.3	4.8	2.7	1.7	2.4	0.6	21.4

Note that percentages do not add up to 100% as respondents could mark all that apply.

Table 6: Additional Certification for Audit Managers and CAEs (%)

Country	Need for Additional Certification beyond CIA for Audit Managers		Need for Additional Certification beyond CIA for CAEs	
	Total Number of Respondents	Frequencies	Total Number of Respondents	Frequencies
Austria	55	65.5	51	68.6
Belgium	20	60.0	18	66.7
Bulgaria	26	46.2	23	43.5
Cyprus	5	80.0	5	60.0
Czech Republic	55	41.8	54	44.4
Estonia	6	16.7	5	20.0
Finland	13	92.3	13	100.0
France	76	85.5	75	77.3
Germany	40	67.5	40	62.5
Greece	14	35.7	13	53.8
Italy	117	65.8	122	59.0
Netherlands	26	50.0	25	56.0
Norway	10	80.0	10	50.0
Poland	8	37.5	7	42.9
Portugal	10	60.0	13	38.5
Romania	4	50.0	4	25.0
Spain	84	75.0	78	78.2
Sweden	17	70.6	21	66.7
Switzerland	15	73.3	14	71.4
Turkey	29	44.8	29	48.3
UK & Ireland	68	73.5	68	69.1
Overall Average	**698**	**65.2**	**688**	**63.1**

Note that only CAEs responded to this question.

1.6.   Professional Experience

According to Table 7, respondents have, on average, 6.9 years of experience in engineering, 6.8 years in management and 6.6 years of experience in internal auditing.

When comparing all 21 countries, we notice (excluding those countries with the number of respondents lower than 5):

- a high average number of years of expertise in **accounting** in Belgium, Estonia, Finland, and Spain;
- a high average number of years of expertise in **engineering** in Czech Republic and France;

- a high average number of years of expertise in **external auditing** in Estonia, Netherlands, Norway and Sweden;
- a high average number of years of expertise in **finance** in Austria, Belgium, Czech Republic, Estonia, France, Norway, Sweden and Switzerland;
- a high average number of years of expertise in **information technology** in Belgium, France and Sweden;
- a high average number of years of expertise in **internal auditing** in Austria, Netherlands, Norway, Switzerland and UK & Ireland;
- a high average number of years of expertise in **management** in Austria, Estonia, Norway, Spain and Sweden;
- a high average number of years of expertise in **other areas** in Estonia and Finland.

Table 7: Professional Experience
(Average number of years)

Country	Accounting	Engineering	External Auditing	Finance	Information Technology	Internal Auditing	Management	Other Areas
Austria	8.3	7.5	4.2	8.6	5.3	10.4	8.0	8.2
Belgium	7.7	5.8	5.5	7.2	7.4	5.6	7.2	5.7
Bulgaria	6.1	1.5	4.8	5.3	6.0	6.8	5.2	5.9
Cyprus	4.8	0.0	4.3	2.9	1.0	5.3	3.1	2.3
Czech Republic	6.8	10.5	4.6	8.6	5.9	4.9	7.7	7.2
Estonia	10.4	2.0	7.0	7.3	4.5	4.2	8.9	9.3
Finland	8.9	1.8	5.3	5.9	6.8	7.0	7.6	7.8
France	6.5	8.3	5.1	7.2	9.3	4.2	6.5	7.3
Germany	5.2	6.1	5.1	3.3	5.0	7.1	6.1	6.3
Greece	4.3	5.9	5.4	5.3	3.0	4.8	6.2	3.1
Italy	6.3	7.6	4.7	5.3	7.1	6.1	6.9	6.9
Netherlands	4.6	3.2	7.8	3.9	4.4	9.0	7.0	6.4
Norway	4.3	0.0	7.2	10.9	6.8	7.6	8.0	6.7
Poland	5.2	3.6	3.1	5.3	3.4	3.5	5.2	5.4
Portugal	6.0	1.5	4.9	6.0	3.7	6.7	6.2	6.6
Romania	9.5	8.8	3.6	6.6	4.7	4.1	3.5	6.7
Spain	7.6	4.6	5.9	5.1	6.1	6.9	7.9	5.7
Sweden	6.2	6.3	9.9	8.3	7.5	7.5	10.1	6.4
Switzerland	6.9	6.7	5.6	7.8	7.0	10.0	6.3	4.3
Turkey	6.2	4.0	6.4	4.9	7.0	6.3	5.3	3.7
UK & Ireland	5.3	4.5	5.8	5.8	6.6	9.0	6.7	6.8
Overall Average	**6.4**	**6.9**	**5.6**	**6.1**	**6.4**	**6.6**	**6.8**	**6.5**

1.7.   Years as Chief Audit Executive

On average, CAEs have been in this position for 6.1 years, ranging from 0 to 44 years.

When comparing all 21 countries, we notice (excluding those countries with the number of respondents lower than 5)

- a high average number of years as CAE in Austria, Netherlands, Sweden and Switzerland;
- a low average number of years as CAE in Czech Republic, France and Poland.

Table 8: Average Number of Years as Chief Audit Executive

Country	Total Number of Respondents	Average Number of Years as CAE	Minimum	Maximum
Austria	57	9.5	0	34
Belgium	21	5.0	1	30
Bulgaria	25	4.5	0	15
Cyprus	6	5.8	4	11
Czech Republic	64	4.3	0	16
Estonia	6	5.8	4	10
Finland	14	4.5	1	10
France	81	4.0	1	17
Germany	41	6.9	1	25
Greece	16	4.8	1	10
Italy	130	5.4	1	24
Netherlands	27	8.6	1	21
Norway	12	6.8	1	18
Poland	8	4.4	0	10
Portugal	17	6.3	1	19
Romania	4	3.5	1	6
Spain	93	6.2	1	44
Sweden	21	12.0	2	36
Switzerland	16	8.4	1	25
Turkey	27	6.1	1	14
UK & Ireland	72	7.0	0	25
Overall Average	**758**	**6.1**		

1.8.   Reporting Status in the Organization

Table 9 shows that 36% of the CAEs describe their internal audit function as being in an independent position reporting to the audit committee, whereas 29% describe their internal audit function as an officer position reporting to executive management.

Table 9: Reporting Status in the Organization (%)

Country	Total Number of Respondents	Staff Position Reporting to a Manager	Managerial Position Reporting to Executive Management	Officer Position Reporting to Executive Management	Independent Position Reporting to the Audit Committee	Other
Austria	58	8.6	10.3	75.9	3.4	1.7
Belgium	21	9.5	9.5	14.3	57.1	9.5
Bulgaria	26	11.5	23.1	34.6	30.8	0.0
Cyprus	6	0.0	50.0	0	50.0	0.0
Czech Republic	65	10.8	58.5	15.4	15.4	0.0
Estonia	6	0.0	33.3	16.7	50.0	0.0
Finland	14	0.0	42.9	14.3	28.6	14.3
France	81	60.5	9.9	4.9	22.2	2.5
Germany	42	4.8	4.8	76.2	7.1	7.1
Greece	16	0.0	31.3	6.3	56.3	6.3
Italy	131	7.6	9.2	26.0	50.4	6.9
Netherlands	28	7.1	35.7	28.6	28.6	0.0
Norway	12	0.0	8.3	0.0	91.7	0.0
Poland	8	0.0	37.5	0.0	62.5	0.0
Portugal	17	5.9	11.8	64.7	5.9	11.8
Romania	4	25.0	25.0	25.0	25.0	0.0
Spain	95	0.0	9.5	50.5	37.9	2.1
Sweden	21	14.3	9.5	4.8	71.4	0.0
Switzerland	16	18.8	6.3	0.0	68.8	6.3
Turkey	31	9.7	25.8	0.0	45.2	19.4
UK & Ireland	71	1.4	21.1	19.7	53.5	4.2
Overall Average	**769**	**12.0**	**18.5**	**29.0**	**36.2**	**4.4**

Note that only CAEs responded to this question.

A comparison between the 21 European countries shows (excluding those countries with the number of respondents lower than 5):

- a high percentage of **staff positions reporting to a manager** in France and Switzerland;
- a high percentage of **managerial positions reporting to executive management** in Cyprus, Czech Republic, Estonia, Finland, Greece, Netherlands and Poland;
- a high percentage of **officer positions reporting to executive management** in Austria, Germany, Portugal and Spain;
- a high percentage of **independent positions reporting to the audit committee or oversight board** in Belgium, Cyprus, Estonia, Greece, Italy, Norway, Poland, Sweden, Switzerland and UK & Ireland.

2 Organizational Characteristics

In the second section of the questionnaire, all respondents were asked to indicate the type of organization they are working for, the geographical location of their organization and the industry in which their organization is operating.

2.1. Type of Organization

Table 10 shows that listed and privately held companies make up for almost 60% of the responding companies. Public sector and governmental organizations represent about one fourth of the respondents. Consultancy organizations as well as not-for-profit organizations are least represented.

Table 10: Type of Organization (%)

Country	Total Number of Respondents	Service Provider / Consultant	Publicly Traded (Listed) Company	Privately Held (Non-Listed) Company	Public Sector / Government	Not-for-profit Organization	Other	Total
Austria	91	16.5	16.5	31.9	22.0	11.0	2.2	100.0
Belgium	102	7.8	42.2	19.6	25.5	2.9	2.0	100.0
Bulgaria	68	5.9	26.5	11.8	42.6	4.4	8.8	100.0
Cyprus	29	10.3	27.6	17.2	31.0	6.9	6.9	100.0
Czech Republic	168	9.5	17.3	25.0	42.9	2.4	3.0	100.0
Estonia	15	13.3	26.7	13.3	46.7	0.0	0.0	100.0
Finland	43	14.0	25.6	25.6	34.9	0.0	0.0	100.0
France	269	6.3	39.0	28.3	17.1	8.6	0.7	100.0
Germany	144	18.1	29.2	34.0	12.5	4.9	1.4	100.0
Greece	76	13.2	59.2	21.1	5.3	0.0	1.3	100.0
Italy	454	12.3	34.6	30.4	20.7	0.9	1.1	100.0
Netherlands	112	6.3	42.9	24.1	20.5	5.4	0.9	100.0
Norway	45	4.4	48.9	8.9	28.9	2.2	6.7	100.0
Poland	83	4.8	15.7	20.5	48.2	3.6	7.2	100.0
Portugal	126	7.9	40.5	22.2	24.6	1.6	3.2	100.0
Romania	40	12.5	10.0	5.0	62.5	0.0	10.0	100.0
Spain	254	6.7	39.0	39.0	11.4	3.1	0.8	100.0
Sweden	67	4.5	32.8	11.9	43.3	3.0	4.5	100.0
Switzerland	33	9.1	60.6	9.1	21.2	0.0	0.0	100.0
Turkey	86	4.7	39.5	34.9	7.0	2.3	11.6	100.0
UK & Ireland	280	6.4	30.7	11.1	43.6	5.7	2.5	100.0
Overall Average	**2,585**	**9.1**	**33.9**	**25.0**	**25.7**	**3.7**	**2.6**	**100.0**

When comparing all 21 countries, we notice:

- a high percentage of **service providers** in Austria, Estonia, Finland, Germany and Greece;
- a high percentage of **publicly traded companies** in Belgium, Greece, Netherlands, Norway and Switzerland;
- a high percentage of **privately held organizations** in Austria, Germany, Italy, Spain and Turkey;
- a high percentage of **public sector / governmental organizations** in Bulgaria, Czech Republic, Estonia, Finland, Poland, Romania, Sweden and UK & Ireland;
- a high percentage of **not-for profit organizations** in Austria, Cyprus, France, Netherlands and UK & Ireland.

Table 11: Geographical Location (%)

Country	Total Number of Respondents	Local	State / Provincial	Regional	National	International / Multinational	Total
Austria	91	9.9	14.3	20.9	15.4	39.6	100.0
Belgium	101	3.0	3.0	5.0	18.8	70.3	100.0
Bulgaria	68	8.8	35.3	4.4	29.4	22.1	100.0
Cyprus	28	17.9	3.6	3.6	50.0	25.0	100.0
Czech Republic	165	13.9	27.3	10.3	17.6	30.9	100.0
Estonia	15	13.3	0.0	0.0	40.0	46.7	100.0
Finland	41	4.9	7.3	2.4	43.9	41.5	100.0
France	267	3.4	0.7	9.7	30.0	56.2	100.0
Germany	144	4.2	7.6	11.1	11.8	65.3	100.0
Greece	73	4.1	1.4	1.4	30.1	63.0	100.0
Italy	457	2.0	.9	6.8	45.1	45.3	100.0
Netherlands	113	1.8	3.5	.9	35.4	58.4	100.0
Norway	45	2.2	4.4	4.4	40.0	48.9	100.0
Poland	83	4.8	18.1	13.3	34.9	28.9	100.0
Portugal	122	1.6	0.0	1.6	51.6	45.1	100.0
Romania	39	2.6	5.1	2.6	69.2	20.5	100.0
Spain	254	1.6	1.2	3.9	28.3	65.0	100.0
Sweden	65	4.6	1.5	1.5	46.2	46.2	100.0
Switzerland	33	6.1	21.2	12.1	6.1	54.5	100.0
Turkey	82	0.0	2.4	6.1	48.8	42.7	100.0
UK & Ireland	281	16.4	2.1	6.4	38.8	36.3	100.0
Overall Average	**2,567**	**5.5**	**5.8**	**6.8**	**34.1**	**47.8**	**100.0**

In general, almost half of the respondents are employed by international / multinational organizations, whereas 34% is employed by a national organization (cf. Table 11).

A comparison of all 21 countries reveals:

- a high percentage of **local organizations** in Cyprus, Czech Republic, Estonia and UK & Ireland;
- a high percentage of **state/provincial organizations** in Austria, Bulgaria, Czech Republic, Poland and Switzerland;
- a high percentage of **regional organizations** in Austria, Germany, Poland and Switzerland;
- a high percentage of **national organizations** in Cyprus, Italy, Portugal, Romania, Sweden and Turkey;
- a high percentage of **multinational companies** in Belgium, Germany Greece, Netherlands and Spain.

2.2.   Industry Classification

Overall, there is more or less an equal spread over all four industries; financial service companies are best represented whereas manufacturing companies are least represented (cf. Table 12).

A comparison between all 21 countries shows:

- a high percentage of **public / governmental sector organizations** in Bulgaria, Czech Republic, Estonia, Poland, Romania, Sweden and UK & Ireland;
- a high percentage of **financial services companies** in Austria, Belgium, Netherlands, Spain, Switzerland and Turkey;
- a high percentage of **non-financial services organizations** in Cyprus, Greece and Portugal;
- a high percentage of **manufacturing companies** in Finland, Germany, Italy, Norway and Turkey.

Table 12: Industry Classification (%)

Country	Total Number of Respondents	Public / Governmental Sector	Financial Services Companies	Non-financial Services Companies	Manufacturing Companies	Total
Austria	85	23.5	36.5	27.1	12.9	100.0
Belgium	99	26.3	37.4	16.2	20.2	100.0
Bulgaria	65	44.6	16.9	18.5	20.0	100.0
Cyprus	29	31.0	6.9	44.8	17.2	100.0
Czech Republic	165	43.6	24.2	16.4	15.8	100.0
Estonia	14	50.0	28.6	21.4	0.0	100.0
Finland	43	34.9	18.6	20.9	25.6	100.0
France	256	18.0	32.0	27.3	22.7	100.0
Germany	140	12.9	32.1	27.1	27.9	100.0
Greece	71	5.6	25.4	50.7	18.3	100.0
Italy	437	21.5	26.1	24.7	27.7	100.0
Netherlands	112	20.5	47.3	18.8	13.4	100.0
Norway	44	29.5	25.0	15.9	29.5	100.0
Poland	77	51.9	22.1	13.0	13.0	100.0
Portugal	123	25.2	26.8	37.4	10.6	100.0
Romania	40	62.5	15.0	22.5	0.0	100.0
Spain	238	12.2	42.0	25.2	20.6	100.0
Sweden	66	43.9	24.2	19.7	12.1	100.0
Switzerland	33	21.2	48.5	18.2	12.1	100.0
Turkey	77	7.8	35.1	28.6	28.6	100.0
UK & Ireland	273	44.7	24.2	20.5	10.6	100.0
Overall Average	**2,487**	**26.7**	**29.6**	**24.3**	**19.3**	**100.0**

3 Internal Audit Function

In the third section of the questionnaire, all respondents were asked to indicate whether their existed an internal audit function in their organization and in case their existed one, the age of this function. Moreover, all respondents were asked to indicate whether a specific list of corporate governance and internal audit documents existed in their organization. Finally, all respondents had to indicate their agreement with a list of statements related to their internal audit function. Besides, CAEs had to reply to questions regarding their appointment and performance evaluation, their relationship with the audit committee (if there existed an audit committee), how the added value of their internal audit function is measured and how the internal audit plan is developed and updated.

3.1. Existence of an Internal Audit Function

Table 13: Existence of an Internal Audit Function (%)

Country	Total Number of Respondents	Frequencies
Austria	91	97.8
Belgium	101	97.0
Bulgaria	69	89.9
Cyprus	29	96.6
Czech Republic	139	96.4
Estonia	15	93.3
Finland	42	92.9
France	270	96.7
Germany	144	98.6
Greece	74	98.6
Italy	458	94.5
Netherlands	113	97.3
Norway	45	86.7
Poland	83	98.8
Portugal	125	92.0
Romania	40	97.5
Spain	256	95.7
Sweden	67	97.0
Switzerland	33	100.0
Turkey	72	91.7
UK & Ireland	281	97.2
Overall Average	**2,547**	**95.8**

The Internal Audit Function (IAF) has been set up in nearly all the respondents' companies (overall average: 96%).

When comparing all the 21 countries, we notice:

- the **highest** presence of internal audit functions in Germany, Greece, Poland and Switzerland;
- the **lowest** presence of internal audit function in Bulgaria, Norway and Turkey.

According to Table 14 the largest numbers of respondents work for IAFs that have been in existence for 0-5 years (34%). Another 23% of the respondents work for IAFs that have been in existence for 6-10 years. A small proportion of the respondents (16%) work in IAFs that have been in existence for 25 or more years.

Table 14: Age of the Internal Audit Function (%)

Country	Total Number of Respondents	0-5 Years	5-10 Years	11-15 Years	16-20 Years	21-25 Years	More than 25 years	Total
Austria	89	21.3	10.1	10.1	11.2	12.4	34.8	100.0
Belgium	88	36.4	21.6	12.5	8.0	9.1	12.5	100.0
Bulgaria	59	81.4	13.6	5.1	0.0	0.0	0.0	100.0
Cyprus	28	46.4	21.4	3.6	0.0	14.3	14.3	100.0
Czech Republic	161	60.9	19.3	14.3	1.9	0.0	3.7	100.0
Estonia	14	35.7	42.9	14.3	0.0	0.0	7.1	100.0
Finland	39	30.8	25.6	10.3	7.7	5.1	20.5	100.0
France	239	23.8	31.0	18.8	12.6	4.2	9.6	100.0
Germany	129	24.8	17.8	7.0	7.8	7.0	35.7	100.0
Greece	72	43.1	27.8	4.2	12.5	0.0	12.5	100.0
Italy	404	45.5	25.0	8.4	6.2	4.7	10.1	100.0
Netherlands	105	17.1	25.7	10.5	6.7	7.6	32.4	100.0
Norway	35	22.9	17.1	5.7	11.4	8.6	34.3	100.0
Poland	78	76.9	19.2	2.6	0.0	0.0	1.3	100.0
Portugal	109	22.9	28.4	13.8	9.2	5.5	20.2	100.0
Romania	37	45.9	35.1	8.1	2.7	8.1	0.0	100.0
Spain	238	21.8	17.2	19.3	19.3	7.6	14.7	100.0
Sweden	61	16.4	32.8	18.0	4.9	4.9	23.0	100.0
Switzerland	33	9.1	0.0	12.1	3.0	6.1	69.7	100.0
Turkey	76	35.5	32.9	13.2	9.2	1.3	7.9	100.0
UK & Ireland	235	17.0	24.7	11.5	14.5	8.5	23.8	100.0
Overall Average	**2,329**	**34.0**	**23.3**	**11.8**	**9.0**	**5.5**	**16.4**	**100.0**

When comparing all 21 countries, we notice:

- a high percentage of **young IAFs** (0-5 years) in Bulgaria, Cyprus, Czech Republic Poland and Romania;
- a high percentage of **mature IAFs** (> 25 years) in Austria, Germany, Netherlands, Norway and Switzerland.

3.2.   Corporate Governance and Internal Audit Documents

According to Table 15, the corporate governance and internal audit documents that are most frequently used are

- Annual Internal Audit Plan / Rolling Audit Plan (82%);
- Internal Audit Charter (70%);
- Internal Audit Risk Assessment (67%).

When comparing all 21 countries, we notice:

- a high percentage of **corporate governance codes** in Netherlands, Norway, Switzerland and UK & Ireland;
- a high percentage of **long term strategic plans** in Finland, Norway, Switzerland and UK & Ireland;
- a high percentage of **audit oversight / committee charters** in Belgium, Netherlands, Switzerland and UK & Ireland;
- a high percentage of **internal audit charters** in Belgium, Estonia, Netherlands and Switzerland;
- a high percentage of **mission statements for the internal audit function** in Belgium, France, Netherlands and Switzerland;
- a high percentage of **internal audit operating manuals / policy statements** in Estonia, Netherlands, Switzerland and UK & Ireland;
- a high percentage of **corporate ethics policies / codes of ethics / codes of conduct** in Belgium, Netherlands, Norway and UK & Ireland;
- a high percentage of **annual internal audit plans / rolling audit plans / quarterly audit plans** in Netherlands, Sweden, Switzerland and UK & Ireland;
- a high percentage of **long term audit plans (longer than 1 year)** in Belgium, Czech Republic, Germany and Switzerland;
- a high percentage of **internal audit risk assessments** in Belgium, Netherlands, Switzerland and UK & Ireland.

Table 15:   Corporate Governance and Internal Audit Documents (%)

Country	Total Number of Respondents	Corporate Governance Code	Strategic Plan Long-term	Audit Committee Charter	Internal Audit Charter	Mission Statement for the Internal Audit Function	Internal Audit Operating Manual /	Code of Ethics / Code of Conduct	Annual Internal Audit Plan / Rolling Audit Plan	Long Term Audit Plan (longer than 1 year)	Internal Audit Risk Assessment
Austria	96	32.3	63.5	13.5	78.1	28.1	61.5	26.0	87.5	41.7	60.4
Belgium	102	62.7	82.4	72.5	90.2	75.5	71.6	82.4	88.2	63.7	85.3
Bulgaria	86	18.6	43.0	4.7	40.7	33.7	44.2	50.0	62.8	34.9	38.4
Cyprus	29	48.3	51.7	44.8	69.0	41.4	37.9	48.3	75.9	20.7	44.8
Czech Republic	186	39.2	62.9	22.6	78.5	17.2	66.7	73.7	86.0	64.0	69.4
Estonia	15	33.3	73.3	26.7	93.3	46.7	73.3	53.3	86.7	40.0	80.0
Finland	43	58.1	86.0	37.2	69.8	46.5	46.5	55.8	83.7	27.9	60.5
France	281	34.9	65.1	49.8	78.3	74.7	53.4	64.4	86.8	35.9	65.1
Germany	157	43.9	66.9	35.0	68.2	34.4	71.3	51.6	77.1	57.3	69.4
Greece	78	50.0	48.7	39.7	69.2	50.0	56.4	52.6	76.9	30.8	50.0
Italy	494	53.0	52.0	42.7	54.9	67.0	55.1	77.9	78.1	32.2	63.6
Netherlands	113	65.5	76.1	63.7	84.1	69.0	75.2	84.1	92.9	55.8	81.4
Norway	45	64.4	88.9	55.6	71.1	55.6	64.4	93.3	84.4	31.1	77.8
Poland	97	24.7	44.3	18.6	62.9	30.9	54.6	44.3	79.4	36.1	67.0
Portugal	136	33.8	48.5	39.7	54.4	47.8	44.1	54.4	78.7	24.3	54.4
Romania	72	15.3	37.5	13.9	43.1	29.2	36.1	40.3	43.1	27.8	40.3
Spain	261	58.2	76.6	56.7	67.8	52.9	66.3	66.7	88.9	42.5	70.5
Sweden	68	45.6	79.4	42.6	82.4	36.8	57.4	57.4	94.1	23.5	80.9
Switzerland	33	63.6	90.9	75.8	97.0	72.7	78.8	63.6	100.0	81.8	90.9
Turkey	92	40.2	38.0	38.0	76.1	50.0	38.0	43.5	66.3	21.7	45.7
UK & Ireland	282	74.1	85.8	81.9	83.7	64.5	80.5	81.6	92.6	52.8	83.3
Overall Average	2,766	48.1	63.9	45.2	69.7	53.2	60.3	65.4	82.4	41.2	66.7

Note that percentages do not add up to 100% as respondents could mark all that apply.

3.3.   Appointment and Performance Evaluation of the CAE

Table 16: Appointment of the CAE (%)

Country	Total Number of Respondents	Chairperson of the Board	Chief Executive Officer	Audit Committee	Chief Financial Officer	Another person reporting to CFO	Other
Austria	58	50.0	46.6	1.7	15.5	3.4	12.1
Belgium	21	33.3	66.7	76.2	33.3	0.0	4.8
Bulgaria	21	42.9	33.3	9.5	4.8	0.0	19.0
Cyprus	6	66.7	33.3	50.0	33.3	0.0	16.7
Czech Republic	64	31.3	56.3	18.8	3.1	0.0	35.9
Estonia	6	50.0	16.7	33.3	16.7	0.0	33.3
Finland	14	14.3	78.6	35.7	14.3	7.1	0.0
France	81	50.6	70.4	38.3	30.9	2.5	7.4
Germany	43	55.8	55.8	4.7	37.2	2.3	2.3
Greece	15	33.3	80.0	26.7	20.0	0.0	0.0
Italy	129	62.8	49.6	27.1	6.2	0.8	9.3
Netherlands	28	25.0	78.6	53.6	32.1	3.6	17.9
Norway	12	58.3	66.7	41.7	8.3	0.0	8.3
Poland	8	62.5	37.5	37.5	12.5	0.0	50.0
Portugal	17	58.8	58.8	11.8	23.5	0.0	5.9
Romania	4	25.0	75.0	25.0	25.0	0.0	0.0
Spain	94	36.2	58.5	51.1	11.7	1.1	7.4
Sweden	21	38.1	42.9	23.8	4.8	0.0	9.5
Switzerland	15	80.0	40.0	60.0	13.3	0.0	13.3
Turkey	32	53.1	34.4	21.9	6.3	0.0	6.3
UK & Ireland	70	12.9	52.9	75.7	64.3	5.7	15.7
Overall Average	**759**	**44.1**	**55.2**	**34.4**	**20.2**	**1.7**	**12.1**

Note that percentages do not add up to 100% as respondents could mark all that apply and only CAEs responded to this question.

In a majority of the cases (55%), the Chief Audit Executive (CAE) is appointed by the Chief Executive Officer (CEO). In many cases (44%), the chairperson of the Board is also involved in the appointment (cf. Table 16).

When comparing all 21 countries, we notice (excluding those countries with the number of respondents lower than 5):

- a high percentage of involvement of the **chairperson of the board** in Cyprus, Italy, Poland and Switzerland;
- a high percentage of involvement of the **Chief Executive Officer** in Finland, Greece, and Netherlands;
- a high percentage of involvement of the **audit committee** in Belgium, Netherlands, Switzerland and UK & Ireland;
- a high percentage of involvement of the **Chief Financial Officer** in Belgium, Cyprus, Germany and UK & Ireland;
- a high percentage of involvement of **another person reporting to CFO** in Austria, Finland, Netherlands and UK & Ireland;
- a high percentage of involvement of **other** persons in Bulgaria, Czech Republic, Estonia and Poland.

Table 17 shows that the Chief Executive Officer's involvement is most prevalent in the CAEs' evaluation (46%) followed by the audit committee (39%) and senior management (27%). When comparing all 21 countries, we notice (excluding those countries with the number of respondents lower than 5):

- a high percentage of involvement of the **board of directors** in Italy, Norway, Portugal and Switzerland;
- a high percentage of involvement of the **chairperson of the Board** in Estonia, Italy and Switzerland;
- a high percentage of involvement of the **Chief Executive Officer** in Finland, France, Greece and Netherlands;
- a high percentage of involvement of the **audit committee** in Belgium, France, Switzerland and UK & Ireland;
- a high percentage of involvement of **senior management** in Estonia, Czech Republic, France and UK & Ireland;
- a high percentage of involvement of the **auditee / client at the end of audit** in Estonia, Sweden and UK & Ireland;
- a high percentage of involvement of the **supervisor (periodically)** in Austria, Estonia and Poland;
- a high percentage of involvement of the **peers / subordinates (periodically)** in Estonia, Switzerland and UK & Ireland.
- a high percentage of **no CAE evaluation** in Greece, Norway, Poland and Sweden.

Table 17: Performance Evaluation of the CAE (%)

Country	Total Number of Respondents	Board of Directors	Chairperson of the Board	Chief Executive Officer	Audit Committee	Senior Management	Auditee	Supervisor periodically	Peers / Subordinates	Not evaluated
Austria	58	29.3	19.0	44.8	6.9	8.6	8.6	17.2	8.6	6.9
Belgium	21	19.0	14.3	52.4	76.2	4.8	9.5	9.5	0.0	4.8
Bulgaria	21	33.3	9.5	23.8	9.5	33.3	4.8	0.0	4.8	0.0
Cyprus	6	33.3	33.3	50.0	50.0	0.0	0.0	0.0	0.0	0.0
Czech Republic	64	29.7	17.2	48.4	21.9	45.3	20.3	14.1	4.7	3.1
Estonia	6	33.3	50.0	16.7	33.3	50.0	50.0	16.7	50.0	0.0
Finland	14	7.1	7.1	71.4	50.0	14.3	21.4	0.0	7.1	0.0
France	81	8.6	33.3	59.3	55.6	42.0	9.9	9.9	8.6	3.7
Germany	43	23.3	23.3	41.9	14.0	14.0	20.9	7.0	7.0	9.3
Greece	15	13.3	33.3	60.0	26.7	20.0	6.7	0.0	0.0	13.3
Italy	129	38.0	37.2	45.0	34.1	20.9	3.1	2.3	0.8	2.3
Netherlands	28	14.3	17.9	53.6	46.4	10.7	17.9	10.7	3.6	7.1
Norway	12	41.7	8.3	33.3	33.3	33.3	25.0	0.0	8.3	16.7
Poland	8	25.0	0.0	37.5	25.0	12.5	25.0	50.0	0.0	12.5
Portugal	17	35.3	17.6	41.2	23.5	5.9	5.9	0.0	0.0	5.9
Romania	4	25.0	0.0	50.0	25.0	25.0	0.0	50.0	0.0	0.0
Spain	94	14.9	20.2	50.0	52.1	25.5	16.0	4.3	1.1	1.1
Sweden	21	33.3	23.8	38.1	33.3	23.8	33.3	9.5	9.5	14.3
Switzerland	15	46.7	60.0	20.0	60.0	33.3	20.0	0.0	13.3	0.0
Turkey	32	18.8	9.4	34.4	21.9	25.0	0.0	0.0	0.0	6.3
UK & Ireland	70	12.9	5.7	44.3	72.9	48.6	28.6	11.4	22.9	2.9
Overall Average	**759**	**23.8**	**22.7**	**46.2**	**38.7**	**26.7**	**13.8**	**7.8**	**6.2**	**4.3**

Note that percentages do not add up to 100% as respondents could mark all that apply and only CAEs responded to this question.

3.4.   Relationship with the Audit Committee

CAEs confirm that an audit / oversight committee exists in 60% of the cases (cf. Table 18).

A comparison of all 21 countries reveals excluding those countries with a number of respondents lower than 5):

- a **high** percentage of audit committees or equivalent in Belgium, France, Netherlands, Switzerland and UK & Ireland;
- a **low** percentage of audit committees or equivalent in Austria, Bulgaria, Czech Republic, Estonia and Germany.

Table 18: Existence of an Audit Committee / Oversight Committee (%)

Country	Total Number of Respondents	Frequencies
Austria	58	24.1
Belgium	21	90.5
Bulgaria	20	25.0
Cyprus	6	66.7
Czech Republic	57	21.1
Estonia	6	33.3
Finland	13	69.2
France	80	81.3
Germany	42	26.2
Greece	14	57.1
Italy	126	59.5
Netherlands	28	85.7
Norway	12	50.0
Poland	8	37.5
Portugal	16	56.3
Romania	4	50.0
Spain	92	76.1
Sweden	21	47.6
Switzerland	15	80.0
Turkey	25	60.0
UK & Ireland	70	95.7
Overall Average	**734**	**60.2**

Note that only CAEs responded to this question.

On average, CAEs attended (entirely or in part) 4.3 meetings of the audit committee during last fiscal year (cf. Table 19).

A comparison of the 21 countries reveals (excluding those countries with a number of respondents lower than 5):

- a **high** average number of meetings attended by the CAE in Italy, Norway Spain, Switzerland and Turkey;
- a **low** average number of meetings attended by the CAE in Austria, Finland, Germany, Netherlands and Sweden.

Table 19: Audit Committee / Oversight Committee Meetings

Country	Number of Audit Committee / Oversight Committee meetings you attended (entirely or in part) during the last fiscal year	
	Total Number of Respondents	Mean
Austria	14	1.8
Belgium	19	4.0
Bulgaria	4	1.5
Cyprus	4	5.0
Czech Republic	20	3.4
Estonia	2	1.5
Finland	9	3.3
France	64	3.6
Germany	9	2.3
Greece	8	3.6
Italy	71	5.7
Netherlands	23	3.0
Norway	6	5.8
Poland	3	2.0
Portugal	9	3.8
Romania	1	10.0
Spain	68	5.0
Sweden	10	3.4
Switzerland	12	5.7
Turkey	16	6.0
UK & Ireland	67	4.0
Overall Average	**439**	**4.3**

Note that this question was only answered by those CAEs who indicated in question 21 (cf. Table 18) that their company has an audit committee.

Of the responding CAEs with audit committees, 54% regularly meet privately with the audit committee / oversight committee / chairperson (cf. Table 20).

When comparing all 21 countries, we notice (excluding those countries with the number of respondents lower than 5):

- a **high** percentage of private meetings in Greece, Sweden, Switzerland Turkey and UK & Ireland;
- a **low** percentage of private meetings in Austria, Finland, France, Germany and Netherlands.

Table 20: Private Meetings with Audit Committee / Oversight Committee / Chairperson (%)

Country	Total Number of Respondents	Frequencies
Austria	14	14.3
Belgium	19	57.9
Bulgaria	5	0.0
Cyprus	4	75.0
Czech Republic	16	62.5
Estonia	2	50.0
Finland	9	33.3
France	65	41.5
Germany	9	22.2
Greece	8	75.0
Italy	73	60.3
Netherlands	23	43.5
Norway	6	50.0
Poland	3	100.0
Portugal	9	44.4
Romania	2	50.0
Spain	69	44.9
Sweden	10	70.0
Switzerland	12	75.0
Turkey	15	73.3
UK & Ireland	67	76.1
Overall Average	**440**	**54.3**

Note that this question was only answered by those CAEs who indicated in question 21 (cf. Table 18) that their company has an audit committee.

Table 21: Appropriate Access to Audit Committee / Oversight Committee (%)

Country	Total Number of Respondents	Frequencies
Austria	14	50.0
Belgium	19	94.7
Bulgaria	5	60.0
Cyprus	4	100.0
Czech Republic	15	86.7
Estonia	2	100.0
Finland	9	88.9
France	63	76.2
Germany	9	77.8
Greece	8	75.0
Italy	73	89.0
Netherlands	23	95.7
Norway	6	100.0
Poland	3	100.0
Portugal	9	100.0
Romania	2	100.0
Spain	68	94.1
Sweden	10	90.0
Switzerland	12	100.0
Turkey	17	82.4
UK & Ireland	66	93.9
Overall Average	**437**	**87.9**

Note that this question was only answered by those CAEs who indicated in question 21 (cf. Table 18) that their company has an audit committee.

It is notable that for those responding companies with an audit committee, 88% of the CAEs believe they have appropriate access to the audit committee (cf. Table 21).

A comparison of all 21 countries (excluding those countries with a number of respondents lower than 5):

- a **high** percentage (100%) of appropriate access to the audit committee / oversight committee in Norway, Portugal and Switzerland;
- a **low** percentage of appropriate access to the audit committee / oversight committee in Austria and Bulgaria;

3.5.   Measurement of Added Value of the Internal Audit Function

According to Table 22, the measures of "added value" with the highest overall average are:

- Recommendations accepted / implemented (48%);
- Reliance by external auditors on the Internal Audit Function (31%);
- Customer / auditee surveys from audited departments (29%).

It has to be marked that 35% of respondents state that they their IAF does not formally measure the added value.

Table 22:   Measurement of Added Value of the Internal Audit Function (%)

Country	Total Number of Respondents	Auditee surveys from audited departments	Recommendations accepted / implemented	Cost savings and improvements from	Number of management requests	Reliance by external auditors on the Internal	Budget to actual audit hours	Cycle time from entrance conference to draft report	Number of major audit findings	Other	No formal measurement of value added
Austria	58	8.6	32.8	20.7	5.2	34.5	12.1	3.4	10.3	5.2	58.6
Belgium	21	33.3	42.9	19.0	28.6	14.3	14.3	14.3	9.5	0.0	42.9
Bulgaria	21	19.0	47.6	47.6	19.0	14.3	0.0	4.8	19.0	19.0	38.1
Cyprus	6	0.0	16.7	33.3	16.7	33.3	16.7	0.0	0.0	16.7	50.0
Czech Republic	64	32.8	46.9	18.8	14.1	15.6	7.8	6.3	37.5	15.6	34.4
Estonia	6	33.3	83.3	0.0	33.3	33.3	50.0	16.7	16.7	16.7	0.0
Finland	14	50.0	21.4	14.3	7.1	21.4	14.3	7.1	7.1	28.6	21.4
France	81	30.9	65.4	14.8	23.5	42.0	11.1	12.3	23.5	8.6	34.6
Germany	43	27.9	25.6	20.9	14.0	27.9	14.0	9.3	9.3	14.0	44.2
Greece	15	26.7	53.3	26.7	13.3	13.3	13.3	6.7	33.3	13.3	33.3
Italy	128	7.8	48.4	22.7	18.0	34.4	7.0	6.3	12.5	14.1	33.6
Netherlands	28	35.7	35.7	10.7	17.9	35.7	21.4	21.4	21.4	10.7	42.9
Norway	12	41.7	25.0	16.7	8.3	25.0	8.3	16.7	8.3	0.0	58.3
Poland	9	22.2	33.3	22.2	11.1	11.1	11.1	11.1	22.2	22.2	44.4
Portugal	17	17.6	64.7	35.3	35.3	11.8	17.6	11.8	17.6	11.8	29.4
Romania	4	25.0	75.0	25.0	0.0	25.0	25.0	25.0	50.0	25.0	0.0
Spain	94	35.1	56.4	21.3	26.6	26.6	9.6	11.7	22.3	7.4	33.0
Sweden	21	57.1	42.9	19.0	14.3	42.9	19.0	19.0	4.8	0.0	23.8
Switzerland	15	46.7	40.0	6.7	20.0	53.3	53.3	33.3	46.7	0.0	33.3
Turkey	32	12.5	62.5	28.1	25.0	15.6	28.1	25.0	34.4	12.5	25.0
UK & Ireland	70	60.0	52.9	8.6	22.9	47.1	24.3	15.7	18.6	22.9	25.7
Overall Average	**759**	**28.5**	**48.2**	**19.8**	**19.0**	**30.6**	**14.0**	**11.3**	**19.6**	**12.0**	**35.4**

Note that percentages do not add up to 100% as respondents could mark all that apply and only CAEs responded to this question.

When comparing all 21 countries, we notice (excluding those countries with a number of respondents lower than 5):

- a high percentage of **customer / auditee surveys** as measure of added value in Finland, Sweden, Switzerland and UK & Ireland;
- a high percentage of **recommendations accepted / implemented** as measure of added value in Estonia, France, Portugal and Turkey;
- a high percentage of **cost savings and improvements from recommendations implemented** as measure of added value in Bulgaria, Cyprus, Portugal and Turkey;
- a high percentage of **number of management requests** as measure of added value in Estonia, Belgium, Portugal and Spain;
- a high percentage of **reliance by external auditors on the internal audit function** as measure of added value in France, Sweden, Switzerland and UK & Ireland;
- a high percentage of **budget to actual audit hours** as measure of added value in Estonia, Switzerland, Turkey and UK & Ireland;
- a high percentage of **cycle time from entrance conference to draft report** as measure of added value in Netherlands, Sweden, Switzerland and Turkey;
- a high percentage of **number of major audit findings** as measure of added value in Czech Republic, Greece, Switzerland and Turkey;
- a high percentage of **other measures of added value** in Bulgaria Finland, Poland and UK & Ireland;
- a high percentage of **no formal measurement of value added** in Austria, Cyprus, Germany, Norway and Poland.

3.6.   Internal Audit Planning

Table 23 shows that 62% of the responding CAEs update their audit planning once a year, whereas 34% update their audit planning multiple times a year

Comparing all 21 countries shows (excluding those countries with a number of respondents lower than 5):

- a high percentage of **multiple updates per year** in Netherlands, Norway, Turkey and UK & Ireland;
- a high percentage of **updates every year** in Bulgaria, Czech Republic, Poland, Romani, Spain;
- a high percentage of **updates every two years** in Belgium, Netherlands, Switzerland and Turkey;
- a high percentage of updates **less than every two years** in Belgium and Cyprus;
- a high percentage of **no use of an audit plan** in Bulgaria, Spain, Turkey and UK & Ireland.

Table 23: Update of Internal Audit Plan (%)

Country	Total Number of Respondents	Multiple times per year	Every year	Every two years	Less than every two years	No audit plan	Total
Austria	56	39.3	57.1	0.0	1.8	1.8	100.0
Belgium	21	28.6	61.9	4.8	4.8	0.0	100.0
Bulgaria	20	15.0	75.0	0.0	0.0	10.0	100.0
Cyprus	6	33.3	50.0	0.0	16.7	0.0	100.0
Czech Republic	64	20.3	79.7	0.0	0.0	0.0	100.0
Estonia	6	33.3	66.7	0.0	0.0	0.0	100.0
Finland	13	30.8	69.2	0.0	0.0	0.0	100.0
France	80	28.8	66.3	0.0	1.3	3.8	100.0
Germany	40	35.0	62.5	0.0	0.0	2.5	100.0
Greece	14	35.7	64.3	0.0	0.0	0.0	100.0
Italy	123	30.1	64.2	0.8	1.6	3.3	100.0
Netherlands	27	48.1	44.4	3.7	0.0	3.7	100.0
Norway	12	58.3	41.7	0.0	0.0	0.0	100.0
Poland	8	25.0	75.0	0.0	0.0	0.0	100.0
Portugal	16	31.3	68.8	0.0	0.0	0.0	100.0
Romania	4	25.0	75.0	0.0	0.0	0.0	100.0
Spain	91	13.2	82.4	0.0	0.0	4.4	100.0
Sweden	20	35.0	65.0	0.0	0.0	0.0	100.0
Switzerland	15	40.0	53.3	6.7	0.0	0.0	100.0
Turkey	29	51.7	37.9	3.4	0.0	6.9	100.0
UK & Ireland	70	67.1	27.1	1.4	0.0	4.3	100.0
Overall Average	**735**	**33.5**	**62.0**	**0.8**	**0.8**	**2.9**	**100.0**

Note that only CAEs responded to this question.

Table 24 shows that 84% of the CAEs use a **risk-based methodology** to determine the audit plan, whereas 73% takes into account **requests from management**.

When comparing all the 21 countries, we notice (excluding those countries with the number of respondents lower than 5):

- a high percentage of **risk-based methodology** to determine the internal audit plan in Belgium, Estonia, Sweden, Switzerland and UK & Ireland;
- a high percentage of **consultation of previous years audit plan** to determine the internal audit plan in Austria, France, Poland and Switzerland;

- a high percentage of **consultation with divisional or business heads** to determine the internal audit plan in Belgium, Estonia, Finland and UK & Ireland;
- a high percentage of **requests from management** having an impact on the internal audit plan in Estonia, Czech Republic, Finland and France;
- a high percentage of **audit committee / oversight committee requests** having an impact on the internal audit plan in Belgium, Netherlands, Switzerland and UK & Ireland;
- a high percentage of **compliance / regulatory requirements** having an impact on the internal audit plan in Belgium, Netherlands, Norway, Poland, Switzerland and Turkey;
- a high percentage of **requests from or consultation with external auditors** having an impact on the internal audit plan in Belgium, Estonia, Switzerland and UK & Ireland;
- a high percentage of **other input** for the audit plan in Czech Republic, Estonia, Netherlands and Poland.

Table 24: Input for the Audit Plan (%)

Country	Total Number of Respondents	Use of a risk-based methodology	Consult previous years audit plan	Consultation with divisional or business heads	Requests from management	Audit Committee / Oversight Committee	Compliance / regulatory requirements	Requests from or consultation with external auditors	Other
Austria	57	87.7	70.2	28.1	68.4	12.3	52.6	40.4	12.3
Belgium	21	95.2	61.9	85.7	81.0	81.0	76.2	52.4	4.8
Bulgaria	19	89.5	26.3	57.9	84.2	21.1	42.1	10.5	0.0
Cyprus	6	66.7	66.7	66.7	50.0	50.0	33.3	16.7	16.7
Czech Republic	64	82.8	65.6	45.3	84.4	14.1	18.8	12.5	21.9
Estonia	6	100.0	66.7	83.3	100.0	33.3	50.0	50.0	16.7
Finland	14	92.9	35.7	85.7	85.7	42.9	14.3	28.6	0.0
France	78	78.2	69.2	78.2	85.9	52.6	42.3	30.8	6.4
Germany	42	90.5	66.7	40.5	69.0	19.0	47.6	47.6	11.9
Greece	15	73.3	53.3	46.7	66.7	26.7	60.0	6.7	0.0
Italy	124	78.2	59.7	36.3	62.9	47.6	60.5	23.4	8.9
Netherlands	27	85.2	55.6	66.7	66.7	70.4	66.7	44.4	18.5
Norway	12	91.7	50.0	66.7	41.7	58.3	66.7	33.3	8.3
Poland	9	88.9	77.8	77.8	66.7	44.4	66.7	11.1	22.2
Portugal	17	82.4	58.8	35.3	82.4	41.2	29.4	17.6	5.9
Romania	4	100.0	50.0	25.0	75.0	25.0	50.0	50.0	0.0
Spain	90	74.4	52.2	60.0	75.6	53.3	62.2	17.8	5.6
Sweden	21	95.2	66.7	81.0	33.3	47.6	19.0	33.3	14.3
Switzerland	15	100.0	80.0	73.3	80.0	73.3	80.0	73.3	6.7
Turkey	30	66.7	53.3	33.3	73.3	46.7	66.7	10.0	13.3
UK & Ireland	67	98.5	56.7	86.6	80.6	77.6	61.2	53.7	7.5
Overall Average	**738**	**83.7**	**60.2**	**56.2**	**73.2**	**45.1**	**51.8**	**29.9**	**9.8**

Note that the percentages do not add up to 100% as respondents could mark all that apply and only CAEs responded to this question.

3.7.   Opinion on the Internal Audit Status

All respondents were asked to evaluate the following Statements:

a. Your Internal Audit Function is an independent objective assurance and consulting activity.
b. Your Internal Audit Function adds value.
c. Internal Audit brings a systematic approach to evaluate the effectiveness of risk management.
d. Your Internal Audit Function brings a systematic approach to evaluate the effectiveness of internal controls.
e. Your Internal Audit Function brings a systematic approach to evaluate the effectiveness of governance processes.
f. Your Internal Audit Function proactively examines important financial matters, risks, and internal controls.
g. Your Internal Audit Function is an integral part of the governance process by providing reliable information to management.
h. The way your Internal Audit Function adds value to the governance process is through direct access to the Audit Committee.
i. Your Internal Audit Function has sufficient status in the organization to be effective.
j. Independence is a key factor for your Internal Audit Function to add value.
k. Objectivity is a key factor for your Internal Audit Function to add value.
l. Your Internal Audit Function is credible within your organization.
m. Compliance with *The IIA's International Standards for the Professional Practice of Internal Auditing* is a key factor for your Internal Audit Function to add value to the governance process.
n. Compliance with The IIA's Code of Ethics is a key factor for your Internal Audit Function to add value to the governance process.

Overall, Table 25 shows that the statements with the highest agreement are:

1. Objectivity is a key factor for your Internal Audit Function to add value (average score of 4.54);
2. Independence is a key factor for your Internal Audit Function to add value (average score of 4.42);
3. Your Internal Audit Function is an independent objective assurance and consulting activity (average score of 4.28);
4. Your Internal Audit Function adds value (average score of 4.26).

When comparing all 21 countries, we notice:

- a high agreement with statement "**a. Your Internal Audit Function is an independent objective assurance and consulting activity**" in Belgium, Estonia, Germany and Switzerland;

53

- a high agreement with statement "**b. Your Internal Audit Function adds value**" in Portugal, Spain, Sweden and Turkey;

- a high agreement with statement "**c. Internal Audit brings a systematic approach to evaluate the effectiveness of risk management**" in Belgium, Germany, Romania and Switzerland;

- a high agreement with statement "**d. Your Internal Audit Function brings a systematic approach to evaluate the effectiveness of internal controls**" in Belgium, Estonia, Germany and Switzerland;

- a high agreement with statement "**e. Your Internal Audit Function brings a systematic approach to evaluate the effectiveness of governance processes**" in Czech Republic, Finland, Norway, Romania and UK & Ireland;

- a high agreement with statement "**f. Your Internal Audit Function proactively examines important financial matters, risks, and internal controls**" in Portugal, Romania, Spain, Switzerland and UK & Ireland;

- a high agreement with statement "**g. Your Internal Audit Function is an integral part of the governance process by providing reliable information to management**" in Finland, Greece, Portugal and UK & Ireland;

- a high agreement with statement "**h. The way your Internal Audit Function adds value to the governance process is through direct access to the Audit Committee**" in Belgium, Greece, Switzerland and UK & Ireland;

- a high agreement with statement "**i. Your Internal Audit Function has sufficient status in the organization to be effective**" in Belgium, Estonia, Germany and Switzerland;

- a high agreement with statement "**j. Independence is a key factor for your Internal Audit Function to add value**" in Austria, Portugal, Spain and Switzerland;

- a high agreement with statement "**k. Objectivity is a key factor for your Internal Audit Function to add value**" in Austria, Belgium Sweden and Switzerland;

- a high agreement with statement "**l. Your Internal Audit Function is credible within your organization**" in Austria, Belgium, Germany, Norway and Switzerland,

- a high agreement with statement "**m. Compliance with The IIA's International Standards for the Professional Practice of Internal Auditing is a key factor for your Internal Audit Function to add value to the governance process**" in Bulgaria, Italy, Norway, Portugal and Romania;

- a high agreement with statement "**n. Compliance with The IIA's Code of Ethics is a key factor for your Internal Audit Function to add value to the governance process**" in Bulgaria, Estonia, Greece and Romania.

Table 25: Opinion on the Internal Audit Status (means)

Country	a	b	c	d	e	f	g	h	i	j	k	l	m	n
Austria	4.44	4.22	3.70	4.33	3.24	4.00	3.80	2.17	4.01	4.58	4.71	4.39	3.61	3.80
Belgium	4.50	4.30	4.17	4.39	3.57	3.76	3.96	3.67	4.09	4.46	4.71	4.25	3.93	4.02
Bulgaria	4.06	3.89	3.82	3.98	3.73	3.86	3.86	3.07	3.72	4.17	4.29	3.83	4.28	4.27
Cyprus	3.97	4.10	3.55	3.90	3.48	3.52	3.76	3.52	3.55	4.38	4.28	3.93	3.86	4.07
Czech Republic	4.29	4.19	4.01	4.24	3.88	3.85	3.98	2.69	3.81	4.22	4.40	4.05	3.84	3.99
Estonia	4.53	4.20	3.80	4.40	3.80	3.73	3.53	2.77	4.27	4.33	4.60	4.07	3.93	4.20
Finland	4.50	4.19	3.93	4.17	3.88	3.83	4.10	3.33	3.98	4.26	4.55	4.14	3.88	4.07
France	4.26	4.27	3.96	4.24	3.42	3.60	3.83	3.54	3.96	4.53	4.67	4.06	3.65	3.74
Germany	4.55	4.20	4.20	4.40	3.40	3.97	3.91	2.88	4.15	4.55	4.61	4.40	3.84	3.82
Greece	4.15	4.21	3.82	4.14	3.68	3.84	4.14	3.68	3.82	4.29	4.49	4.14	3.89	4.14
Italy	4.08	4.24	4.00	4.16	3.72	3.74	3.81	3.58	3.71	4.45	4.53	3.88	3.95	4.05
Netherlands	4.34	4.32	3.82	4.14	3.60	3.82	3.78	3.62	3.96	4.13	4.40	4.09	3.60	3.72
Norway	4.50	4.34	3.95	4.32	3.93	3.98	3.84	3.63	4.00	4.50	4.57	4.32	3.95	4.00
Poland	3.87	4.02	3.52	4.05	3.42	3.65	3.57	2.38	3.87	3.88	4.05	3.78	3.84	3.80
Portugal	4.17	4.45	3.88	4.32	3.47	4.09	4.06	3.32	3.77	4.64	4.63	4.24	4.04	4.04
Romania	4.41	4.36	4.15	4.33	3.97	4.08	4.03	3.30	4.00	4.50	4.54	4.18	4.18	4.38
Spain	4.44	4.37	4.08	4.28	3.63	4.14	3.94	3.57	3.91	4.61	4.68	4.15	3.76	3.88
Sweden	4.41	4.42	3.73	4.20	3.80	3.76	3.62	3.02	3.58	4.53	4.71	4.14	3.92	4.11
Switzerland	4.73	4.33	4.21	4.39	3.67	4.18	3.91	3.76	4.48	4.64	4.82	4.45	3.91	4.03
Turkey	4.24	4.41	3.95	4.09	3.78	3.86	4.03	3.40	3.71	4.35	4.47	3.97	3.91	4.01
UK & Ireland	4.26	4.24	4.05	4.32	3.92	4.08	4.13	3.76	3.76	4.28	4.42	4.00	3.72	3.78
Overall Average	**4.28**	**4.26**	**3.97**	**4.24**	**3.65**	**3.87**	**3.90**	**3.37**	**3.86**	**4.42**	**4.54**	**4.08**	**3.84**	**3.93**

1 = Strongly Disagree, 2 = Disagree, 3 = Neutral, 4 = Agree, 5 = Strongly Agree

4 Internal Audit Staffing

In the fourth section of the questionnaire, all respondents were asked to indicate the number of staff members working in their internal audit function (per hierarchical level) as well as their average number of training hours over the last 36 months. Besides, CAEs has to indicate which special incentives they use to hire internal audit professionals, the methods they use to make up for staff vacancies, how they compensate missing skill sets, the percentage of internal audit activities as well as the specific activities currently outsourced / co-sourced (including the expected evolution) and the methods used for staff evaluation.

4.1. Number of Staff Members

Table 26: Average Staff Level (FTE means)

Country	Total Number of Respondents	CAE	Managers	Supervisors	Staff	External Auditors	Contract Audit Staff	Support Staff	Total
Austria	82	1.2	2.0	4.2	5.9	4.3	2.3	2.5	8.5
Belgium	92	2.8	9.3	9.7	60.6	2.2	8.5	2.8	66.3
Bulgaria	61	1.0	1.6	3.9	4.0	5.3	10.5	1.0	6.0
Cyprus	28	1.4	1.4	1.4	2.7	1.3	1.0	1.1	5.3
Czech Republic	162	1.2	2.7	2.8	11.3	11.7	1.5	1.8	12.4
Estonia	15	1.3	1.5	1.3	4.5	3.5	1.0	4.0	6.6
Finland	40	1.4	1.9	3.0	6.8	3.5	1.0	4.0	8.0
France	250	3.0	2.7	5.0	23.1	8.8	5.8	6.1	29.3
Germany	131	4.0	5.7	10.9	56.7	8.9	5.8	6.1	59.2
Greece	68	3.0	2.7	4.9	20.7	3.8	2.3	3.0	23.1
Italy	400	1.9	8.4	16.3	55.1	8.6	58.3	9.0	71.5
Netherlands	106	3.6	17.0	32.3	69.2	19.1	5.0	9.8	98.9
Norway	39	3.2	3.8	9.4	18.9	15.5	2.3	5.3	26.6
Poland	76	1.0	1.3	3.1	11.9	4.2	15.0	1.3	11.9
Portugal	115	1.3	3.8	5.9	47.8	5.0	2.1	6.9	55.4
Romania	35	2.3	3.1	4.3	28.6	1.0	6.0	5.1	36.0
Spain	239	2.1	3.9	9.2	33.9	3.7	3.9	3.2	39.5
Sweden	65	1.1	2.6	7.4	22.9	3.3	6.0	2.9	24.3
Switzerland	33	2.5	4.2	7.3	12.3	2.0	2.0	2.2	21.7
Turkey	77	4.3	1.8	4.5	18.0	22.1	2.0	5.6	23.6
UK & Ireland	260	3.0	8.9	11.6	19.0	8.3	4.1	4.8	38.0
Overall Average	**2,374**	**2.4**	**6.0**	**10.2**	**32.6**	**7.6**	**18.8**	**5.8**	**41.5**

Table 26 shows that the responding internal audit functions have, on average, 42 FTE. Staff members (juniors) represent the largest proportion, followed by contract audit staff (outsourcing or co-sourcing) and supervisors (seniors).

When comparing the total number of FTE between all 21 countries, we notice:

* a **high** total number of FTE in Belgium, Germany, Italy, Netherlands and Portugal;
* a **low** total number of FTE in Austria, Bulgaria, Cyprus, Czech Republic, Estonia, Finland, Greece, Poland, Sweden, Switzerland and Turkey.

4.2.   Incentives

According to Table 27, the four most indicated special incentives to hire internal audit professionals are:

* Other (20%);
* Transportation allowance (13%);
* Relocation expenses (10%);
* Vehicle provided by organization (10%).

Table 27: Special Incentives to Hire Internal Audit Professionals (%)

Country	Total Number of Respondents	Relocation expenses	Signing bonus	Stock options	Accelerated rises	Vehicle provided by organization	Transportation allowance	Other
Austria	56	3.6	0.0	3.6	1.8	3.6	12.5	16.1
Belgium	20	15.0	5.0	5.0	10.0	25.0	15.0	15.0
Bulgaria	28	0.0	3.6	0.0	0.0	10.7	3.6	39.3
Cyprus	6	0.0	0.0	0.0	0.0	16.7	50.0	16.7
Czech Republic	64	1.6	1.6	1.6	3.1	6.3	4.7	15.6
Estonia	6	0.0	0.0	0.0	0.0	33.3	0.0	33.3
Finland	14	0.0	7.1	0.0	0.0	7.1	0.0	0.0
France	81	8.6	7.4	7.4	8.6	9.9	11.1	8.6
Germany	43	30.2	2.3	2.3	2.3	4.7	23.3	20.9
Greece	16	12.5	12.5	6.3	0.0	18.8	18.8	18.8
Italy	131	17.0	6.1	3.8	5.3	6.9	8.4	17.6
Netherlands	27	22.2	14.8	0.0	11.1	25.9	33.3	25.9

Table 27: Special Incentives to Hire Internal Audit Professionals (%)

Country	Total Number of Respondents	Relocation expenses	Signing bonus	Stock options	Accelerated rises	Vehicle provided by organization	Transportation allowance	Other
Norway	12	25.0	8.3	8.3	0.0	16.7	16.7	8.3
Poland	8	12.5	0.0	0.0	0.0	0.0	25.0	50.0
Portugal	17	11.8	5.9	11.8	0.0	11.8	17.6	35.3
Romania	4	0.0	0.0	0.0	0.0	25.0	0.0	75.0
Spain	96	2.1	2.1	3.1	13.5	4.2	10.4	31.3
Sweden	21	9.5	0.0	0.0	4.8	4.8	4.8	33.3
Switzerland	15	20.0	6.7	6.7	6.7	6.7	13.3	13.3
Turkey	32	9.4	0.0	0.0	9.4	25.0	37.5	28.1
UK & Ireland	69	17.4	1.4	5.8	4.3	14.5	13.0	13.0
Overall Average	**766**	**10.3**	**4.0**	**3.7**	**5.7**	**9.9**	**13.1**	**20.4**

Note that percentages do not add up to 100% as respondents could indicate all that apply and only CAEs responded to this question.

When comparing all 21 countries, we notice (excluding those countries with the number of respondents lower than 5):

- a high percentage of **relocation expenses** in Germany, Netherlands, Norway and Switzerland;
- a high percentage of **signing bonuses** in Greece, Netherlands and Norway;
- a high percentage of **stock options** in France, Greece, Norway, Portugal and Switzerland;
- a high percentage of **accelerated rises** in Belgium, Netherlands and Spain;
- a high percentage of **vehicles provided by the organization** in Belgium, Estonia, Greece, Netherlands and Turkey;
- a high percentage of **transportation allowance** in Cyprus, Netherlands and Turkey;
- a high percentage of **other incentives** in Bulgaria, Poland and Portugal.

4.3.   Vacancies and Missing Skill Sets

About one third (33%) of the responding CAEs indicate that they had no vacancies at the time they completed the questionnaire (2006). Table 28 shows that the three most common methods to make up for staff vacancies are:

- Reduce areas of coverage (29%);
- Co-sourcing from internal audit service providers (25%);
- Borrowing staff from other departments (14%).

A comparison between all 21 European countries reveals (excluding those countries with the number of respondents lower than 5):

- a high percentage of **control self assessment facilitations** as a method to make up for staff vacancies in Belgium, Estonia, Germany and Italy;
- a high percentage of **reduced areas of coverage** as a method to make up for staff vacancies in France, Poland, Portugal and UK & Ireland;
- a high percentage of **increased use of audit software** as a method to make up for staff vacancies in Belgium, Greece, Netherlands and Turkey;
- a high percentage of **borrowing staff from other departments** as a method to make up for staff vacancies in Greece, Norway and Poland;
- a high percentage of **co-sourcing from internal audit service providers** as a method to make up for staff vacancies in Belgium, France, Norway, Portugal and UK & Ireland;
- a high percentage of **other methods** to make up for staff vacancies in Netherlands, Poland, Sweden and Turkey.

Note the high **absence of vacancies** in Austria, Bulgaria, Estonia, Finland and Switzerland.

Only a small proportion of the responding CAEs (13%) indicate that they had no missing skills sets at the time they completed the questionnaire (2006). Furthermore, Table 29 shows that the three most common methods to compensate for missing skill sets are:

- co-sourcing / outsourcing (49%);
- borrowing staff from other departments (20%);
- reduce areas of coverage (18%)

Comparing all 21 countries shows (excluding those countries with the number of respondents lower than 5):

- a high percentage of **reduced areas of coverage** to compensate for missing skill sets in Czech Republic, Finland, France and Greece;
- a high percentage of **more reliance on audit software** to compensate for missing skill sets in Greece, Poland, Portugal, Turkey and UK & Ireland;
- a high percentage of **borrowing staff from other departments** to compensate for missing skill sets in Czech Republic, Finland, Poland and Switzerland;
- a high percentage of **co-sourcing / outsourcing** to compensate for missing skill sets in Belgium, Finland, Norway, Switzerland and UK & Ireland;
- a high percentage of **other methods** to compensate for missing skill sets in Bulgaria, Czech Republic, Estonia, Poland and Turkey.

Note the high **absence of missing skill sets** in Germany, Netherlands and Switzerland.

Table 28: Methods to make up for Staff Vacancies (%)

Country	Total Number of Respondents	Facilitate Control Self Assessments	Reduce areas of coverage	Increased use of audit software	Borrowing staff from other departments	Co-sourcing from internal audit service providers	No vacancies	Other
Austria	56	8.9	21.4	16.1	10.7	10.7	42.9	5.4
Belgium	20	15.0	25.0	30.0	15.0	35.0	25.0	10.0
Bulgaria	28	7.1	10.7	10.7	10.7	7.1	64.3	17.9
Cyprus	6	0.0	16.7	0.0	0.0	33.3	33.3	16.7
Czech Republic	64	10.9	21.9	4.7	15.6	9.4	53.1	7.8
Estonia	6	16.7	0.0	16.7	0.0	33.3	66.7	16.7
Finland	14	14.3	14.3	7.1	0.0	14.3	42.9	0.0
France	81	11.1	45.7	1.2	16.0	38.3	29.6	6.2
Germany	43	16.3	23.3	16.3	18.6	25.6	27.9	4.7
Greece	16	6.3	12.5	25.0	25.0	31.3	25.0	0.0
Italy	131	15.3	26.7	16.8	19.1	28.2	19.1	19.1
Netherlands	27	3.7	29.6	18.5	11.1	25.9	33.3	22.2
Norway	12	8.3	33.3	0.0	33.3	58.3	8.3	0.0
Poland	8	0.0	37.5	12.5	25.0	25.0	25.0	25.0
Portugal	17	5.9	41.2	17.6	5.9	41.2	23.5	5.9
Romania	4	24.0	50.0	0.0	0.0	25.0	25.0	0.0
Spain	96	7.3	33.3	13.5	8.3	15.6	29.2	20.8
Sweden	21	4.8	23.8	0.0	14.3	28.6	28.6	33.3
Switzerland	15	0.0	20.0	0.0	6.7	20.0	80.0	6.7
Turkey	32	12.5	9.4	18.8	6.3	12.5	37.5	25.0
UK & Ireland	69	7.2	46.4	11.6	15.9	36.2	26.1	14.5
Overall Average	**766**	**10.2**	**28.7**	**12.1**	**14.0**	**24.5**	**32.8**	**13.6**

Note that percentages do not add up to 100% as respondents could mark all that apply and only CAEs responded to this question.

Table 29: Compensation for Missing Skill Sets (%)

Country	Total Number of Respondents	Reduce areas of coverage	More reliance on audit software	Borrowing staff from other departments	Co-sourcing / Outsourcing	No missing skill sets	Other
Austria	56	7.1	7.1	23.2	53.6	14.3	16.1
Belgium	20	5.0	10.0	20.0	65.0	5.0	10.0
Bulgaria	28	25.0	10.7	25.0	25.0	10.7	28.6
Cyprus	6	16.7	0.0	0.0	50.0	16.7	16.7
Czech Republic	64	28.1	0.0	29.7	35.9	7.8	25.0
Estonia	6	16.7	0.0	0.0	50.0	16.7	33.3
Finland	14	28.6	7.1	28.6	64.3	0.0	0.0
France	81	27.2	2.5	24.7	59.3	12.3	8.6
Germany	43	18.6	4.7	16.3	48.8	25.6	4.7
Greece	16	31.3	12.5	25.0	37.5	12.5	6.3
Italy	131	18.3	5.3	26.7	37.4	14.5	18.3
Netherlands	27	14.8	0.0	18.5	59.3	18.5	14.8
Norway	12	25.0	0.0	16.7	66.7	8.3	0.0
Poland	8	25.0	12.5	37.5	37.5	12.5	25.0
Portugal	17	17.6	11.8	17.6	58.8	0.0	0.0
Romania	4	25.0	0.0	0.0	75.0	25.0	0.0
Spain	96	9.4	9.4	9.4	49.0	13.5	16.7
Sweden	21	19.0	4.8	23.8	42.9	9.5	23.8
Switzerland	15	13.3	6.7	33.3	86.7	26.7	6.7
Turkey	32	12.5	18.8	3.1	34.4	12.5	43.8
UK & Ireland	69	14.5	11.6	11.6	63.8	11.6	10.1
Overall Average	**766**	**17.9**	**6.7**	**20.1**	**49.1**	**13.1**	**15.8**

Note that percentages do not add up to 100% as respondents could mark all that apply. Note that only CAEs responded to this question.

4.4. Outsourcing and Co-Sourcing

Table 30 indicates that the majority of the responding internal audit functions (73%) currently outsource less than 10% of their activities. The remaining 27% currently outsource more than 10% of their activities.

Table 30: Percentage of Internal Audit Activities Currently Outsourced / Co-Sourced (%)

Country	Total Number of Respondents	0 – 10 %	11 – 20 %	21 – 30 %	> 30 %	Total
Austria	55	69.1	21.8	5.5	3.6	100.0
Belgium	19	57.9	21.1	10.5	10.6	100.0
Bulgaria	27	85.2	7.4	3.7	3.7	100.0
Cyprus	4	50.0	25.0	25.0	0.0	100.0
Czech Republic	61	82.0	4.9	6.6	6.4	100.0
Estonia	4	50.0	25.0	25.0	0.0	100.0
Finland	12	50.0	8.3	33.3	8.3	100.0
France	81	76.5	11.1	6.2	6.1	100.0
Germany	40	72.5	17.5	2.5	7.5	100.0
Greece	14	64.3	0.0	21.4	14.2	100.0
Italy	125	74.4	12.0	5.6	8.0	100.0
Netherlands	26	69.2	19.2	0.0	11.5	100.0
Norway	11	63.6	18.2	9.1	9.1	100.0
Poland	8	75.0	12.5	12.5	0.0	100.0
Portugal	16	50.0	6.3	25.0	18.9	100.0
Romania	4	25.0	50.0	0.0	25.0	100.0
Spain	93	80.6	10.8	4.3	4.4	100.0
Sweden	20	65.0	15.0	10.0	10.0	100.0
Switzerland	15	73.3	13.3	6.7	6.7	100.0
Turkey	29	89.7	3.4	0.0	6.9	100.0
UK & Ireland	62	64.5	12.9	8.1	14.4	100.0
Overall Average	**726**	**73.0**	**12.4**	**6.9**	**7.2**	**100.0**

Note that only the CAEs responded to this question.

Comparing all 21 European countries shows (excluding those countries with the number of respondents lower than 5):

- a **low** percentage of internal audit activities currently outsourced / co-sourced (less than 10%) in Bulgaria, Czech Republic, Spain and Turkey;
- a **high** percentage of internal audit activities currently outsourced / co-sourced (more than 10%) in Belgium, Finland, Greece, Norway, Portugal, Sweden and UK & Ireland.

Table 31 shows that more than half of the responding CAEs (56%) expect that the proportion of outsourced / co-sourced internal audit activities will remain the same in the upcoming years. In contrast, 36% expect the proportion of outsourced / co-sourced internal audit activities to increase in the upcoming years.

Table 31: Evolution of Outsourced / Co-Sourced Activities (%)

Country	Total Number of Respondents	Increase	Decrease	Remain the Same	Total
Austria	47	38.3	4.3	57.4	100.0
Belgium	20	40.0	10.0	50.0	100.0
Bulgaria	22	27.3	4.5	68.2	100.0
Cyprus	5	20.0	20.0	60.0	100.0
Czech Republic	48	37.5	6.3	56.3	100.0
Estonia	6	33.3	16.7	50.0	100.0
Finland	13	23.1	15.4	61.5	100.0
France	75	36.0	6.7	57.3	100.0
Germany	40	27.5	7.5	65.0	100.0
Greece	14	28.6	0.0	71.4	100.0
Italy	109	33.9	12.8	53.2	100.0
Netherlands	26	30.8	7.7	61.5	100.0
Norway	12	33.3	0.0	66.7	100.0
Poland	8	12.5	0.0	87.5	100.0
Portugal	14	50.0	7.1	42.9	100.0
Romania	3	66.7	33.3	0.0	100.0
Spain	83	49.4	4.8	45.8	100.0
Sweden	18	38.9	5.6	55.6	100.0
Switzerland	15	33.3	6.7	60.0	100.0
Turkey	23	34.8	8.7	56.5	100.0
UK & Ireland	67	31.3	11.9	56.7	100.0
Overall Average	**668**	**35.8**	**8.1**	**56.1**	**100.0**

Note that only the CAEs responded to this question.

When comparing all 21 European countries, we notice (excluding those countries with the number of respondents lower than 5):

- a high percentage of CAEs expecting an **increase** in the proportion of outsourced / co-sourced internal audit activities in Belgium, Portugal and Spain;
- a high percentage of CAEs expecting a **decrease** in the proportion of outsourced / co-sourced internal audit activities in Cyprus, Estonia, Finland and Italy;
- a high percentage of CAEs expecting the proportion of outsourced / co-sourced internal audit activities to **remain the same** in Bulgaria, Germany, Greece, Norway and Poland.

Table 32: What Type of Activities are Outsourced (%)

Country	Total Number of Respondents	Administrative (audit plan, assign tasks)	Business Viability Assessments	Compliance with Privacy Policies	Compliance with Corporate Governance and Regulatory Code	Control Framework Monitoring and Development	Corporate Takeovers / Mergers	Enterprise Risk Management	Ethics Audits	External Audit Assistance	Health, Safety and Environment	Financial Auditing	Information Risk Assessment	Information Technology Department Assessment
Austria	83	1.2	1.2	1.2	1.2	0.0	2.4	0.0	1.2	0.0	1.2	4.8	4.8	4.8
Belgium	92	0.0	0.0	0.0	1.1	1.1	9.8	0.0	1.1	10.9	2.2	28.3	2.2	12.0
Bulgaria	80	3.8	3.8	2.5	2.5	2.5	1.3	2.5	0.0	17.5	6.3	26.3	7.5	6.3
Cyprus	27	3.7	7.4	0.0	3.7	3.7	7.4	3.7	0.0	29.6	11.1	22.2	22.2	33.3
Czech Republic	174	0.0	2.3	0.0	1.1	1.7	3.4	1.7	0.6	1.1	2.3	24.7	10.9	15.5
Estonia	14	0.0	0.0	7.1	7.1	7.1	0.0	7.1	7.1	14.3	14.3	64.3	28.6	42.9
Finland	42	0.0	2.4	0.0	4.8	4.8	4.8	2.4	0.0	2.4	0.0	31.0	9.5	11.9
France	252	1.2	1.6	1.2	1.6	1.2	8.3	1.6	1.2	15.1	2.8	32.1	7.1	10.7
Germany	127	0.0	0.8	3.1	0.8	0.0	1.6	0.8	0.0	0.0	4.7	4.7	3.1	2.4
Greece	73	2.7	0.0	2.7	2.7	0.0	2.7	2.7	1.4	24.7	6.8	32.9	11.0	11.0
Italy	440	0.7	0.9	0.5	1.1	1.1	3.4	2.3	0.2	1.6	1.8	7.7	6.8	7.5
Netherlands	99	0.0	2.0	0.0	2.0	0.0	7.1	0.0	0.0	10.1	4.0	34.3	5.1	8.1
Norway	36	0.0	0.0	0.0	0.0	0.0	2.8	0.0	0.0	13.9	5.6	50.0	2.8	5.6
Poland	86	1.2	4.7	2.3	2.3	3.5	8.1	2.3	1.2	3.5	8.1	30.2	19.8	16.3
Portugal	119	0.0	0.8	0.0	0.8	0.8	2.5	0.8	0.0	5.0	2.5	31.1	0.8	5.0
Romania	64	0.0	1.6	1.6	1.6	1.6	3.1	0.0	0.0	18.8	3.1	25.0	1.6	0.0
Spain	238	0.4	0.8	2.1	0.4	0.4	1.3	0.4	0.0	2.5	2.5	32.4	13.9	13.4
Sweden	58	0.0	0.0	0.0	1.7	1.7	1.7	0.0	3.4	0.0	3.4	29.3	3.4	5.2
Switzerland	32	0.0	0.0	0.0	0.0	0.0	3.1	0.0	0.0	6.3	3.1	18.8	3.1	12.5
Turkey	77	3.9	5.2	0.0	3.9	2.6	14.3	5.2	0.0	14.3	3.9	31.2	5.2	7.8
UK & Ireland	253	1.6	1.2	1.2	1.6	1.2	2.8	1.6	2.8	10.7	3.2	19.0	4.0	9.5
Overall Average	**2,466**	**0.9**	**1.5**	**1.1**	**1.5**	**1.2**	**4.3**	**1.5**	**0.8**	**7.4**	**3.3**	**23.1**	**7.3**	**9.6**

Country	Internal Control Testing / Systems Evaluation	Investigations of Fraud and Irregularities	Linkage of Strategy and Company Performance	Management Effectiveness Audit	Operational Audits	Project Management	Quality assessment of internal audit activity	Quality / ISO audits	Resource Management and Controls	Security Issues	Social and Sustainability Audits	Special Projects	Technical Competency Training for Auditors
Austria	2.4	2.4	1.2	3.6	0.0	1.2	15.7	2.4	1.2	1.2	0.0	1.2	10.8
Belgium	4.3	5.4	2.2	3.3	3.3	8.7	23.9	17.4	2.2	1.1	3.3	9.8	30.4
Bulgaria	6.3	6.3	1.3	8.8	3.8	2.5	20.0	15.0	3.8	3.8	3.8	3.8	5.0
Cyprus	7.4	0.0	0.0	0.0	3.7	0.0	7.4	14.8	11.1	7.4	11.1	11.1	25.9
Czech Republic	2.3	3.4	0.6	3.4	1.1	4.6	17.2	4.0	1.1	4.6	4.6	14.4	19.5
Estonia	14.3	0.0	7.1	14.3	0.0	14.3	42.9	14.3	7.1	21.4	7.1	35.7	57.1
Finland	11.9	11.9	0.0	2.4	7.1	2.4	26.2	23.8	0.0	7.1	7.1	28.6	31.0
France	5.2	5.6	1.2	2.4	2.4	4.8	21.0	11.1	2.4	4.0	5.2	6.7	39.7
Germany	2.4	3.9	0.8	1.6	0.0	0.0	3.9	1.6	0.0	2.4	1.6	3.1	3.1
Greece	1.4	4.1	1.4	1.4	4.1	2.7	16.4	16.4	1.4	4.1	1.4	11.0	24.7
Italy	1.4	2.7	0.5	1.1	0.2	2.0	6.4	7.0	0.9	1.6	0.9	2.7	15.9
Netherlands	5.1	6.1	1.0	0.0	0.0	5.1	14.1	5.1	1.0	4.0	3.0	7.1	36.4
Norway	8.3	8.3	0.0	2.8	2.8	2.8	33.3	13.9	0.0	8.3	5.6	13.9	33.3
Poland	4.7	9.3	2.3	5.8	2.3	5.8	8.1	7.0	5.8	9.3	1.2	14.0	16.3
Portugal	1.7	2.5	0.8	5.0	0.8	0.0	5.9	6.7	0.0	3.4	2.5	5.9	11.8
Romania	1.6	4.7	1.6	4.7	0.0	0.0	14.1	7.8	0.0	1.6	6.3	1.6	14.1
Spain	4.6	0.8	0.4	0.8	1.7	1.3	9.2	17.2	0.0	4.2	6.7	5.0	22.7
Sweden	1.7	5.2	1.7	8.6	1.7	1.7	32.8	17.2	0.0	6.9	5.2	6.9	36.2
Switzerland	3.1	6.3	0.0	3.1	3.1	3.1	28.1	3.1	3.1	6.3	3.1	6.3	34.4
Turkey	1.3	3.9	2.6	3.9	1.3	7.8	1.3	16.9	6.5	11.7	2.6	10.4	24.7
UK & Ireland	2.8	3.2	2.4	5.1	2.8	4.0	30.4	11.5	2.8	5.9	4.3	11.5	37.5
Overall Average	3.4	4.0	1.1	3.0	1.6	3.1	15.2	10.1	1.7	4.2	3.5	7.5	23.5

Table 32 shows the activities that are most frequently outsourced:

- Technical Competency Training for Auditors (24%);
- Financial Auditing (23%);
- Quality assessment of internal audit activity (15%);
- Quality / ISO audits (10%).

When comparing all 21 countries, we notice:

- a high percentage of outsourcing of **administrative (audit plan, assign tasks) activities** in Bulgaria, Cyprus and Turkey;
- a high percentage of outsourcing of **business viability assessments** in Cyprus, Poland and Turkey;
- a high percentage of outsourcing of **compliance with privacy policies** in Estonia, Germany and Greece;
- a high percentage of outsourcing of **compliance with corporate governance and regulatory code requirements** in Estonia, Finland and Turkey;
- a high percentage of outsourcing of **control framework monitoring and development** in Cyprus, Estonia and Finland;
- a high percentage of outsourcing of **corporate takeovers / mergers** in Belgium, France and Turkey;
- a high percentage of outsourcing of **Enterprise Risk Management** in Cyprus, Estonia and Turkey;
- a high percentage of outsourcing of **ethics audits** in Estonia, Sweden and UK & Ireland;
- a high percentage of outsourcing of **external audit assistance** in Cyprus, Greece and Romania;
- a high percentage of outsourcing of **health, safety and environment** in Cyprus, Estonia and Poland;
- a high percentage of outsourcing of **financial auditing** in Estonia, Netherlands and Norway;
- a high percentage of outsourcing of **information risk assessments** in Cyprus, Estonia and Poland;
- a high percentage of outsourcing of **information technology department assessments** in Cyprus, Estonia and Poland;
- a high percentage of outsourcing of **internal control testing / systems evaluation** in Estonia, Finland and Norway;
- a high percentage of outsourcing of **investigations of fraud and irregularities** in Finland, Norway and Poland;
- a high percentage of outsourcing of **linkage of strategy and company performance** in Estonia, Turkey and UK & Ireland;
- a high percentage of outsourcing of **management effectiveness audit** in Bulgaria, Estonia and Sweden;
- a high percentage of outsourcing of **operational audits** in Bulgaria, Finland and Greece;

- a high percentage of outsourcing of **project management** in Belgium, Estonia and Turkey;
- a high percentage of outsourcing of **quality assessments of internal audit activity** in Estonia, Norway and Sweden;
- a high percentage of outsourcing of **quality / ISO audits** in Belgium, Finland and Sweden;
- a high percentage of outsourcing of **resource management and controls** in Cyprus, Estonia and Turkey;
- a high percentage of outsourcing of **security issues** in Estonia, Poland and Turkey;
- a high percentage of outsourcing of **social and sustainability audits** in Cyprus, Estonia and Finland;
- a high percentage of outsourcing of **special projects** in Czech Republic, Estonia and Finland;
- a high percentage of outsourcing of **technical competency training for auditors** in Estonia, France and UK & Ireland.

Table 33: What Type of Activities are Co-sourced (%)

Country	Total Number of Respondents	Administrative (audit plan, assign tasks)	Business Viability Assessments	Compliance with Privacy Policies	Compliance with Corporate Governance and Regulatory Code	Control Framework Monitoring and Development	Corporate Takeovers / Mergers	Enterprise Risk Management	Ethics Audits	External Audit Assistance	Health, Safety and Environment	Financial Auditing	Information Risk Assessment	Information Technology Department Assessment
Austria	83	1.2	2.4	3.6	0.0	3.6	4.8	4.8	1.2	2.4	3.6	14.5	19.3	27.7
Belgium	92	0.0	6.5	9.8	8.7	9.8	9.8	6.5	3.3	7.6	7.6	6.5	8.7	8.7
Bulgaria	80	0.0	0.0	1.3	0.0	2.5	0.0	0.0	0.0	1.3	0.0	1.3	3.8	2.5
Cyprus	27	0.0	7.4	0.0	3.7	3.7	11.1	3.7	0.0	7.4	3.7	14.8	3.7	0.0
Czech Republic	174	1.7	1.1	1.7	0.6	0.6	1.7	0.6	2.3	1.1	0.6	2.3	6.9	6.9
Estonia	14	0.0	7.1	0.0	7.1	0.0	0.0	0.0	0.0	0.0	0.0	0.0	7.1	14.3
Finland	42	0.0	4.8	7.1	7.1	0.0	4.8	4.8	7.1	7.1	2.4	4.8	16.7	14.3
France	252	1.6	10.7	13.1	17.1	12.3	8.7	17.1	4.0	3.2	12.3	8.3	11.1	10.7
Germany	127	2.4	1.6	0.8	0.8	3.9	5.5	0.0	3.1	2.4	3.1	16.5	12.6	8.7
Greece	73	1.4	8.2	1.4	5.5	4.1	5.5	6.8	1.4	8.2	6.8	8.2	6.8	6.8
Italy	440	1.8	1.4	3.4	3.0	3.6	3.9	5.9	1.4	1.8	3.2	2.7	5.2	3.0
Netherlands	99	0.0	1.0	4.0	4.0	8.1	5.1	8.1	2.0	7.1	3.0	8.1	10.1	6.1
Norway	36	0.0	2.8	11.1	8.3	8.3	5.6	2.8	0.0	0.0	2.8	8.3	11.1	11.1
Poland	86	7.0	11.6	10.5	10.5	15.1	5.8	14.0	8.1	12.8	7.0	5.8	16.3	14.0
Portugal	119	0.8	5.9	3.4	3.4	0.0	5.9	2.5	0.0	1.7	3.4	10.1	5.9	14.3
Romania	64	1.6	1.6	1.6	1.6	3.1	1.6	3.1	3.1	1.6	1.6	1.6	6.3	4.7
Spain	238	0.4	5.0	4.2	5.9	2.1	8.4	4.6	1.7	2.1	4.6	10.9	16.4	14.3
Sweden	58	3.4	3.4	1.7	8.6	6.9	3.4	8.6	6.9	8.6	3.4	3.4	5.2	6.9
Switzerland	32	0.0	6.3	6.3	6.3	9.4	12.5	6.3	6.3	0.0	3.1	6.3	12.5	18.8
Turkey	77	5.2	15.6	7.8	11.7	7.8	10.4	10.4	5.2	13.0	9.1	3.9	3.9	9.1
UK & Ireland	253	0.8	4.0	2.8	5.1	5.1	3.6	4.3	1.6	6.3	3.6	4.7	6.7	7.5
Overall Average	**2,466**	**1.5**	**4.6**	**4.7**	**5.6**	**5.2**	**5.4**	**6.1**	**2.5**	**4.0**	**4.5**	**6.6**	**9.1**	**9.0**

Country	Internal Control Testing / Systems Evaluation	Investigations of Fraud and Irregularities	Linkage of Strategy and Company Performance	Management Effectiveness Review / Audit	Operational Audits	Project Management	Quality assessment of internal audit activity	Quality / ISO audits	Resource Management and Controls	Security Issues	Social and Sustainability Audits	Special Projects	Technical Competency Training for Auditors
Austria	9.6	2.46	7.2	3.6	3.6	3.6	8.4	2.4	2.4	3.6	0.0	9.6	20.5
Belgium	4.3	12.0	1.1	1.1	1.1	7.6	1.1	6.5	7.6	6.5	5.4	10.9	4.3
Bulgaria	2.5	2.5	0.0	0.0	0.0	0.0	2.5	1.3	0.0	0.0	0.0	0.0	0.0
Cyprus	3.7	7.4	0.0	0.0	0.0	0.0	0.0	3.7	0.0	0.0	3.7	3.7	0.0
Czech Republic	1.1	1.7	0.6	0.6	1.1	4.6	1.7	1.1	0.6	0.0	0.0	4.0	2.9
Estonia	7.1	0.0	0.0	0.0	0.0	0.0	0.0	0.0	7.1	7.1	14.3	14.3	7.1
Finland	9.5	4.8	2.4	2.4	7.1	2.4	2.4	2.4	4.8	9.5	2.4	16.7	9.5
France	10.3	14.3	12.3	11.5	7.5	13.9	4.8	9.5	13.9	15.1	6.3	17.9	5.6
Germany	4.7	11.0	5.5	4.7	3.9	4.7	18.1	9.4	0.0	2.4	0.0	7.9	27.6
Greece	4.1	5.5	2.7	2.7	4.1	6.8	1.4	4.1	5.5	4.1	1.4	15.1	6.8
Italy	2.5	2.5	2.5	1.8	2.0	2.7	3.0	1.4	1.4	3.0	0.7	3.9	3.9
Netherlands	4.0	9.1	7.1	3.0	1.0	4.0	3.0	3.0	4.0	8.1	5.1	12.1	12.1
Norway	2.8	2.8	2.8	2.8	0.0	0.0	0.0	2.8	0.0	8.3	2.8	13.9	5.6
Poland	5.8	23.3	16.3	5.8	4.7	17.4	14.0	11.6	12.8	16.3	7.0	17.4	9.3
Portugal	9.2	4.2	3.4	2.5	4.2	5.0	5.0	8.4	0.8	6.7	4.2	15.1	18.5
Romania	1.6	1.6	1.6	3.1	0.0	1.6	1.6	3.1	1.6	1.6	4.7	3.1	4.7
Spain	9.2	3.4	1.7	2.1	0.4	3.4	2.9	8.8	0.8	5.9	5.0	10.5	8.0
Sweden	5.2	5.2	5.2	1.7	0.0	1.7	5.2	5.2	0.0	5.2	3.4	10.3	1.7
Switzerland	0.0	12.5	3.1	3.1	0.0	3.1	31.3	9.4	6.3	6.3	6.3	12.5	28.1
Turkey	5.2	6.5	5.2	7.8	7.8	14.3	5.2	6.5	5.2	9.1	7.8	14.3	6.5
UK & Ireland	4.0	5.9	2.4	3.6	1.6	5.9	5.5	2.8	4.7	7.1	2.4	12.6	7.5
Overall Average	5.2	6.4	4.3	3.5	2.7	5.6	5.0	5.0	3.9	6.0	3.1	10.1	8.2

Table 33 shows the activities that are most frequently co-sourced:

- Special Projects (10%);
- Information Risk Assessment (9%);
- Information Technology Department Assessment (9%);
- Technical Competency Training for Auditors (8%).

When comparing all 21 countries, we notice:

- a high percentage of co-sourcing of **administrative (audit plan, assign tasks) activities** in Poland, Sweden and Turkey;
- a high percentage of co-sourcing of **business viability assessments** in France, Poland and Turkey;
- a high percentage of co-sourcing of **compliance with privacy policies** in France, Norway and Poland;
- a high percentage of co-sourcing of **compliance with corporate governance and regulatory code requirements** in France, Poland, and Turkey;
- a high percentage of co-sourcing of **control framework monitoring and development** in Belgium, France and Poland;
- a high percentage of co-sourcing of **corporate takeovers / mergers** in Cyprus, Switzerland and Turkey;
- a high percentage of co-sourcing of **Enterprise Risk Management** in France, Poland and Turkey;
- a high percentage of co-sourcing of **ethics audits** in Finland, Poland and Sweden;
- a high percentage of co-sourcing of **external audit assistance** in Poland, Sweden and Turkey;
- a high percentage of co-sourcing of **health, safety and environment** in Belgium, France and Turkey;
- a high percentage of co-sourcing of **financial auditing** in Austria, Cyprus and Germany;
- a high percentage of co-sourcing of **information risk assessments** in Austria, Finland and Spain;
- a high percentage of co-sourcing of **information technology department assessments** in Austria, Finland and Switzerland;
- a high percentage of co-sourcing of **internal control testing / systems evaluation** in Austria, Finland and France;
- a high percentage of co-sourcing of **investigations of fraud and irregularities** in France, Poland and Switzerland;
- a high percentage of co-sourcing of **linkage of strategy and company performance** in Austria, France and Poland;
- a high percentage of co-sourcing of **management effectiveness audit** in France, Poland and Turkey;
- a high percentage of co-sourcing of **operational audits** in Finland, France and Turkey;

- a high percentage of co-sourcing of **project management** in France, Poland and Turkey;
- a high percentage of co-sourcing of **quality assessments of internal audit activity** in Germany, Poland and Switzerland;
- a high percentage of co-sourcing of **quality / ISO audits** in France, Germany, Poland, Switzerland;
- a high percentage of co-sourcing for **Resource Management and Controls** in Belgium, France and Poland;
- a high percentage of co-sourcing of **security issues** in Finland, France and Poland;
- a high percentage of co-sourcing of **social and sustainability audits** in Estonia, Turkey and Poland;
- a high percentage of co-sourcing of **special projects** in Finland, France and Poland;
- a high percentage of co-sourcing of **technical competency training for auditors** in Austria, Germany and Switzerland.

4.5.   Staff Evaluation

Table 34 shows that 73% of the responding CAEs indicate that staff evaluation is periodically done by the supervisor. About 40% indicate that auditee feedback is also used as a method of staff evaluation.

Table 34:   Methods of Staff Evaluation (%)

Country	Total Number of Respondents	By supervisor periodically	Auditee feedback	Peers / subordinates periodically	Other
Austria	56	80.4	30.4	10.7	12.5
Belgium	20	80.0	35.0	15.0	5.0
Bulgaria	28	32.1	35.7	14.3	46.4
Cyprus	6	66.7	16.7	33.3	0.0
Czech Republic	64	84.4	42.2	15.6	14.1
Estonia	6	66.7	66.7	33.3	50.0
Finland	14	50.0	57.1	14.3	14.3
France	81	81.5	37.0	19.8	3.7
Germany	43	86.0	44.2	18.6	7.0
Greece	16	56.3	18.8	0.0	12.5
Italy	131	54.2	26.0	5.3	23.7
Netherlands	27	88.9	40.7	25.9	14.8
Norway	12	58.3	58.3	41.7	25.0
Poland	8	62.5	62.5	25.0	25.0
Portugal	17	82.4	23.5	5.9	11.8
Romania	4	100.0	50.0	0.0	50.0
Spain	96	77.1	50.0	17.7	26.0
Sweden	21	85.7	52.4	28.6	14.3
Switzerland	15	93.3	60.0	6.7	13.3
Turkey	32	59.4	25.0	25.0	15.6
UK & Ireland	69	87.0	59.4	31.9	7.2
Overall Average	**766**	**73.2**	**39.9**	**16.8**	**16.6**

Note that percentages do not add up to 100% as respondents could mark
all that apply and CAEs responded to this question.

Comparing all 21 European countries shows (excluding those countries with the number of respondents lower than 5):

- A high percentage of periodic staff evaluation by the **supervisor** in Germany, Netherlands, Sweden, Switzerland and UK & Ireland;
- A high percentage of staff evaluation based on **auditee feedback** in Estonia, Finland, Norway, Poland, Switzerland and UK & Ireland;
- A high percentage of periodic staff evaluation by **peers / subordinates** in Cyprus, Estonia, Norway and UK & Ireland.

4.6.   Training

On average, respondents received 132 hours of formal training over the last 36 months (cf. Table 35).

Table 35: Average Number of Hours of Training over the Last 36 Months (means)

Country	Total Number of Respondents	Mean
Austria	90	67.2
Belgium	98	175.5
Bulgaria	63	125.4
Cyprus	29	124.8
Czech Republic	161	184.6
Estonia	15	194.9
Finland	41	127.7
France	258	96.4
Germany	142	75.6
Greece	71	110.4
Italy	437	115.2
Netherlands	111	203.8
Norway	41	163.0
Poland	83	169.6
Portugal	120	141.0
Romania	39	355.0
Spain	247	153.5
Sweden	62	101.0
Switzerland	32	115.8
Turkey	81	108.4
UK & Ireland	272	113.5
Overall Average	**2,493**	**131.6**

Comparing all 21 countries shows:

- the **highest** number of training hours in Czech Republic, Estonia, Netherlands and Romania.
- the **lowest** number of training hours in Austria, France and Germany.

5 Internal Auditing Standards

In the fifth section of the questionnaire, all respondents were asked whether they use the IIA Standards (in whole or in part) as well as the reasons for not using the IIA Standards. Moreover, all respondents had to evaluate the adequacy of all IIA Standards as well as the Practice Advisories and indicate whether they comply with each of the IIA Standards. Finally, all respondents were asked to indicate whether they are compliant with Standard 1300, 1311 and 1312 (quality assessment and improvement) and which activities are part of their quality assessment and improvement program.

5.1. Overall Use of IIA Standards

Overall, about 80% of the respondents state to use (in whole or in part) the IIA Standards. In all 21 countries, the percentage of usage (in whole or in part) lies above 50%.

Table 36: Overall Use of IIA Standards (in Whole or in Part) (%)

Country	Total number of respondents	Frequency
Austria	90	66.7
Belgium	101	87.1
Bulgaria	65	73.8
Cyprus	29	51.7
Czech Republic	143	91.6
Estonia	15	100.0
Finland	41	95.1
France	269	68.8
Germany	139	85.6
Greece	73	74.0
Italy	445	83.8
Netherlands	112	71.4
Norway	44	79.5
Poland	82	91.5
Portugal	120	71.7
Romania	38	89.5
Spain	254	78.7
Sweden	67	85.1
Switzerland	33	97.0
Turkey	65	66.2
UK & Ireland	279	79.6
Total	**2,504**	**79.5**

When comparing the 21 countries, we notice:
- the **highest** percentage of use of IIA Standards in Estonia, Czech Republic, Finland, Poland and Switzerland;
- the **lowest** percentage of use of IIA Standards in Cyprus, France and Turkey.

Table 37: Reasons for not using the IIA Standards (%)

Country	Total Number of respondents	Standards or Practice Advisories are too complex	Not appropriate for small organizations	Too costly to comply	Too time consuming	Superseded by local / government regulations or standards	Not appropriate for my industry	Compliance not supported by management/board	Not perceived as adding value by management / board	Inadequate Internal Audit Function staff	Compliance not expected in my country	Other
Austria	88	21.6	25.0	12.5	21.6	10.2	6.8	23.9	13.6	12.5	9.1	9.1
Belgium	94	10.6	14.9	12.8	18.1	6.4	5.3	16.0	18.1	6.4	6.4	10.6
Bulgaria	84	2.4	3.6	3.6	3.6	13.1	3.6	9.5	8.3	21.4	3.6	0.0
Cyprus	29	6.9	17.2	13.8	27.6	0.0	6.9	27.6	17.2	37.9	17.2	20.7
Czech Republic	175	12.0	9.7	6.3	13.7	14.9	6.9	6.9	14.3	6.9	1.7	4.0
Estonia	14	0.0	21.4	7.1	14.3	7.1	0.0	7.1	14.3	7.1	0.0	7.1
Finland	42	9.5	28.6	7.1	19.0	4.8	2.4	16.7	11.9	7.1	0.0	16.7
France	259	13.9	17.0	10.4	18.1	14.7	5.0	17.4	25.9	5.4	6.6	6.9
Germany	134	14.2	25.4	6.0	14.9	7.5	5.2	20.9	20.9	8.2	8.2	12.7
Greece	73	6.9	16.4	8.2	8.2	8.2	2.7	21.9	11.0	21.9	19.2	4.1
Italy	447	6.9	10.7	11.4	11.9	7.8	2.5	15.7	20.6	19.7	3.1	7.8
Netherlands	101	4.9	11.9	5.9	16.8	14.9	2.0	10.9	16.8	7.9	5.0	22.8
Norway	42	2.4	4.8	7.1	11.9	11.9	2.4	7.1	7.1	9.5	2.4	14.3
Poland	88	5.7	8.0	12.5	13.6	13.6	2.3	21.6	15.9	0.0	8.0	8.0
Portugal	125	1.6	2.4	7.2	8.8	1.6	0.8	16.0	8.0	12.8	20.8	7.2
Romania	69	1.5	0.0	2.9	0.0	10.1	1.4	5.8	2.9	5.8	5.8	4.3
Spain	242	6.6	8.7	7.9	12.8	9.9	2.9	11.2	16.1	2.9	5.0	12.4
Sweden	59	8.5	1.7	3.4	11.9	8.5	1.7	10.2	8.5	15.3	11.9	20.3
Switzerland	33	18.2	18.2	15.2	30.3	18.2	9.1	12.1	12.1	6.1	3.0	3.0
Turkey	80	6.3	13.8	15.0	16.3	16.3	6.3	32.5	23.8	36.3	12.5	6.3
UK & Ireland	259	2.3	5.8	2.7	9.3	19.3	4.2	7.3	9.7	7.3	3.9	15.4
Overall average	**2,537**	**7.9**	**11.5**	**8.4**	**13.3**	**11.2**	**3.8**	**14.6**	**16.0**	**11.4**	**6.5**	**9.8**

Note that percentages do not add up to 100% as respondents could mark all that apply.

According to Table 37, the most common reasons for not using the IIA Standards are:

- Management of the organization does not perceive compliance with the IIA Standards as adding value (16%);
- Compliance with the IIA Standards is not supported by management (15%);
- Compliance with the IIA Standards is too time consuming (13%);
- Compliance with the IIA Standards is not appropriate for small organizations (12%);
- Inadequate internal audit function staff to comply with the IIA Standards (11%);
- Compliance with the IIA Standards superseded by local / government regulations or standards (11%).

A comparison between the 21 countries shows:

- a high percentage for **Standards or Practice Advisories are too complex** in Austria, France, Germany and Switzerland;
- a high percentage for Standards or Practice Advisories **not appropriate for small organizations** in Austria, Cyprus, Estonia, Finland, Germany and Switzerland;
- a high percentage for **too costly to comply** with Standards or Practice Advisories in Cyprus, Switzerland and Turkey;
- a high percentage for **too time consuming** to comply with Standards or Practice Advisories in Austria, Cyprus, Finland and Switzerland;
- a high percentage for compliance with Standards or Practice Advisories **superseded by local / government regulations or standards** in Switzerland, Turkey and UK & Ireland;
- a high percentage for compliance with Standards or Practice Advisories **not appropriate for my industry** in Cyprus, Czech Republic and Switzerland.
- a high percentage for **compliance not supported by the management/board of the organization** in Austria, Cyprus, Germany, Poland and Turkey;
- a high percentage for **Standards are not perceived to add value by the management / board of the organization** in France, Germany, Italy and Turkey;
- a high percentage for compliance **inadequate IA function staff** to comply with **Standards or Practice Advisories** in Bulgaria, Cyprus, Greece, Italy and Turkey;
- a high percentage for **compliance not expected in my country** in Cyprus, Greece and Portugal;

5.2. Adequacy and Compliance with IIA Standards

According to Table 38, most respondents believe that the guidance provided by the IIA Standards is adequate. The guidance provided by the Attribute Standards seems to be more adequate than the guidance provided by the Performance Standards. Overall, the Standards that are considered as most adequate are:

- AS 1100 Independence and Objectivity (92%);
- AS 1200 Proficiency and Due Professional Care (90%);
- AS 1000 Purpose, Authority and Responsibilities (90%).

In contrast, Performance Standard 2600 (Management's Acceptance of Risks) and Attribute Standard 1300 (Quality Assurance and Improvement Program) are considered as the least adequate.

Table 38: Adequacy of Guidance Provided by IIA Standards (%)

Country	Total Number of respondents	1000 - Purpose, Authority and Responsibility	1100 - Independence and Objectivity	1200 - Proficiency and Due Professional Care	1300 - Quality Assurance and Improvement	2000 - Managing the Internal Audit Activity	2100 - Nature of work	2200 - Engagement Planning	2300 - Performing the Engagement	2400 - Communicating Results	2500 - Monitoring Progress	2600 - Resolution of Management's Acceptance of Risks
Austria	52	86.5	90.4	90.4	58.8	90.2	78.0	80.4	80.0	82.0	76.5	69.4
Belgium	78	97.4	94.9	97.5	85.5	96.2	92.2	92.2	94.9	94.8	90.9	79.2
Bulgaria	42	95.2	95.1	95.1	87.5	95.1	87.8	92.7	97.6	95.1	87.5	84.6
Cyprus	14	71.4	85.7	92.9	57.1	71.4	78.6	71.4	64.3	78.6	71.4	57.1
Czech Republic	129	90.7	92.4	86.3	76.3	81.7	70.5	89.3	84.5	86.0	81.5	61.5
Estonia	10	100.0	100.0	90.0	100.0	100.0	100.0	90.0	90.0	100.0	100.0	100.0
Finland	36	91.7	91.7	86.1	66.7	86.1	80.6	86.1	85.7	82.9	75.0	80.0
France	154	91.6	91.6	91.5	75.7	86.8	87.3	86.7	86.7	87.9	81.6	78.7
Germany	93	94.6	97.8	95.7	80.0	87.9	83.3	80.4	84.3	90.1	88.8	76.4
Greece	42	85.7	88.1	81.0	76.2	78.6	76.7	81.0	80.5	88.1	89.7	68.3
Italy	314	94.9	95.5	96.8	73.8	92.9	93.1	94.8	94.8	94.8	92.5	73.6
Netherlands	68	76.5	80.6	76.5	76.5	79.4	76.9	78.5	79.7	80.3	79.1	73.1
Norway	27	88.9	88.9	88.9	81.5	88.0	80.0	80.8	76.9	88.5	80.0	73.1
Poland	64	95.3	96.8	95.4	78.1	93.8	89.1	89.2	92.2	92.2	86.9	78.1
Portugal	70	90.0	90.0	88.6	81.2	79.4	84.1	84.1	88.4	82.1	82.6	73.9
Romania	26	96.2	96.0	88.5	84.0	80.8	92.0	92.3	92.3	84.6	92.3	80.8
Spain	185	87.6	92.9	87.4	80.2	85.4	88.3	88.3	88.8	88.7	82.7	81.4
Sweden	47	93.6	95.8	95.7	83.3	83.3	89.6	91.5	89.1	95.7	83.3	78.7
Switzerland	32	96.9	100.0	96.9	87.5	96.9	90.6	93.8	93.8	96.9	93.8	75.0
Turkey	44	88.6	88.6	85.7	65.1	75.0	77.3	74.4	72.1	75.0	72.7	60.0
UK & Ireland	190	80.5	82.6	82.6	72.0	77.5	73.1	77.4	77.0	79.3	77.8	72.7
Overall average	**1,717**	**90.2**	**91.9**	**90.3**	**76.4**	**86.3**	**84.3**	**86.8**	**86.9**	**88.1**	**84.5**	**74.5**

Note that the number of respondents per country is only given for the first Standard as there are very slight differences for the other Standards.

When comparing the 21 countries we notice:

- a high percentage of adequacy of **AS 1000 (Purpose, Authority and Responsibilities)** in Belgium, Bulgaria, Estonia, Germany, Poland, Sweden and Switzerland;
- a high percentage of adequacy of **AS 1100 (Independency and Objectivities)** in Belgium, Bulgaria, Estonia, Poland, Romania and Switzerland;
- a high percentage of adequacy of **AS 1200 (Proficiency and Due Professional Care)** in Bulgaria, Germany, Poland, Romania and Switzerland;
- a high percentage of adequacy of **AS 1300 (Quality Assurance and Improvement Program)** in Belgium, Bulgaria, Estonia and Switzerland;
- a high percentage of adequacy of **PS 2000 (Managing the IAA)** in Belgium, Bulgaria, Estonia, Poland and Switzerland;
- a high percentage of adequacy of **PS 2100 (Nature of Work)** in Belgium, Estonia, Italy, Romania and Switzerland;
- a high percentage of adequacy of **PS 2200 (Engagement Planning)** in Belgium, Bulgaria, Italy, Romania and Switzerland;
- a high percentage of adequacy of **PS 2300 (Performing the Engagement)** in Belgium, Bulgaria, Italy, Poland and Switzerland;
- a high percentage of adequacy of **PS 2400 (Communicating Results)** in Belgium, Bulgaria, Estonia, Sweden and Switzerland;
- a high percentage of adequacy of **PS 2500 (Monitoring Progress)** in Belgium, Estonia, Italy, Romania and Switzerland;
- a low percentage of adequacy of **PS 2600 (Management's Acceptance of Risks)** in Austria, Cyprus, Czech Republic, Greece and Turkey.

It is shown in Table 39 that for all IIA Standards, the level of full compliance is lower than 70%. Particularly, the IIA Standards with a highest degree of compliance are:

- AS 1100 Independence and Objectivity (67%);
- PS 2400 Communicating Results (62%);
- AS 1000 Purpose, Authority and Responsibilities (61%);
- AS 1200 Proficiency and Due Professional Care (59%).

Table 39: Full Compliance with IIA Standards (%)

Country	Total Number of respondents	1000 - Purpose, Authority and Responsibility	1100 - Independence and Objectivity	1200 - Proficiency and Due Professional Care	1300 - Quality Assurance and Improvement	2000 - Managing the Internal Audit Activity	2100 - Nature of work	2200 - Engagement Planning	2300 - Performing the Engagement	2400 - Communicating Results	2500 - Monitoring Progress	2600 - Resolution of Management's Acceptance of Risks
Austria	51	47.1	53.8	46.2	19.6	51.0	30.6	37.3	42.0	50.0	41.2	22.0
Belgium	76	71.1	76.6	61.0	38.7	53.2	58.4	63.6	63.6	68.4	63.6	48.7
Bulgaria	44	70.5	63.6	70.5	57.1	65.9	56.8	60.5	68.2	74.4	50.0	41.9
Cyprus	14	50.0	50.0	71.4	21.4	53.8	64.3	42.9	46.2	50.0	50.0	35.7
Czech Republic	129	58.9	63.1	48.5	37.7	52.3	46.5	61.5	53.1	59.1	50.0	33.3
Estonia	12	66.7	66.7	58.3	36.4	75.0	33.3	58.3	33.3	58.3	41.7	58.3
Finland	38	65.8	71.1	55.3	31.6	55.3	55.3	51.4	42.1	55.3	43.2	39.5
France	149	62.4	60.4	54.1	34.2	43.9	49.7	52.1	57.8	58.8	46.6	39.2
Germany	85	56.5	75.3	59.3	33.7	58.8	44.0	41.7	53.7	61.9	51.2	38.1
Greece	44	63.6	63.6	51.2	40.9	58.1	46.5	46.5	54.5	62.8	58.5	40.9
Italy	313	62.3	69.0	58.6	28.9	55.0	60.7	59.4	61.7	65.7	46.8	34.9
Netherlands	68	61.8	70.1	68.7	31.3	54.4	58.5	56.1	49.2	59.7	47.8	47.0
Norway	28	64.3	71.4	63.0	32.1	60.7	48.1	48.1	53.6	66.7	44.4	35.7
Poland	68	47.1	65.2	56.7	23.1	34.3	35.4	53.0	51.6	58.2	33.8	21.5
Portugal	65	47.7	67.7	67.2	46.8	54.0	42.2	57.8	57.8	57.8	43.8	28.6
Romania	31	64.5	67.7	38.7	38.7	63.3	56.7	56.7	50.0	56.7	64.5	40.0
Spain	178	64.6	70.0	63.5	46.3	53.7	60.1	63.5	61.7	66.1	53.4	42.9
Sweden	48	58.3	64.6	60.4	22.9	48.9	43.8	45.8	45.8	52.1	31.3	37.5
Switzerland	32	65.6	78.1	68.8	53.1	71.9	61.3	67.7	77.4	84.4	71.9	50.0
Turkey	47	57.4	64.6	63.8	34.8	50.0	54.3	58.7	56.3	61.7	48.9	34.8
UK & Ireland	181	63.0	63.4	66.3	37.4	56.5	51.4	58.4	55.9	61.7	50.0	48.0
Overall average	**1.706**	**61.0**	**66.9**	**59.4**	**35.5**	**53.7**	**52.3**	**56.3**	**56.7**	**62.3**	**49.0**	**38.6**

Note that the number of respondents per country is only given for the first Standard as there are very slight differences for the other Standards.

When comparing all 21 countries the results show:

- a high percentage of full compliance with **AS 1000 (Purpose, Authority and Responsibilities)** in Belgium, Bulgaria, Estonia, Finland and Switzerland;
- a high percentage of full compliance with **AS 1100 (Independency and Objectivity)** in Belgium, Finland, Germany, Netherlands, Norway and Switzerland;
- a high percentage of full compliance with **AS 1200 (Proficiency and Due Professional Care)** in Bulgaria, Cyprus, Netherlands, Portugal and Switzerland;
- a high percentage of full compliance with **AS 1300 (Quality Assessment and Improvement Program)** in Bulgaria, Portugal, Spain and Switzerland;
- a high percentage of full compliance with **PS 2000 (Managing the IAA)** in Bulgaria, Estonia, Germany, Romania and Switzerland;
- a high percentage of full compliance with **PS 2100 (Nature of Work)** in Cyprus, Italy, Netherlands, Spain and Switzerland;
- a high percentage of full compliance with **PS 2200 (Engagement Planning)** in Belgium, Bulgaria, Italy, Spain and Switzerland;
- a high percentage of full compliance with **PS 2300 (Performing the Engagement)** in Belgium, Bulgaria, Italy, Spain and Switzerland;
- a high percentage of full compliance with **PS 2400 (Communicating Result)** in Belgium, Bulgaria, Norway, Spain and Switzerland;
- a high percentage of full compliance with **PS 2500 (Monitoring Progress)** in Belgium, Greece, Romania and Switzerland;
- a high percentage of full compliance with **PS 2600 (Management's Acceptance of Risks)** in Belgium, Estonia and Switzerland.

5.3.   Adequacy of Practice Advisories

According to Table 40, the Practice Advisories that are considered as the most adequate are:

- PA 1100 Independency and Objectivity (87%);
- PA 1000 Purpose, Authority and Responsibilities (87%);
- PA 1200 Proficiency and due Professional Care (86%).

Table 40: Adequacy of Practice Advisories (%)

Country	Total Number of respondents	1000 - Purpose, Authority and Responsibility	1100 - Independence and Objectivity	1200 - Proficiency and Due Professional Care	1300 - Quality Assurance and Improvement	2000 - Managing the Internal Audit Activity	2100 - Nature of work	2200 - Engagement Planning	2300 - Performing the Engagement	2400 - Communicating Results	2500 - Monitoring Progress	2600 - Resolution of Management's Acceptance of Risks
Austria	34	82.4	84.8	81.8	75.8	75.0	73.3	78.1	81.3	84.8	84.4	56.3
Belgium	58	82.8	75.4	80.7	69.0	78.6	78.9	71.9	78.9	78.6	78.9	70.2
Bulgaria	37	100.0	97.3	97.4	91.7	100.0	97.1	94.4	100.0	100.0	86.5	81.1
Cyprus	11	90.9	100.0	90.9	81.8	81.8	81.8	81.8	72.7	72.7	54.5	54.5
Czech Republic	108	95.4	91.7	88.6	76.7	82.7	72.8	89.7	83.5	83.8	78.6	57.3
Estonia	11	81.8	90.9	100.0	90.0	90.9	100.0	90.9	90.9	90.9	90.9	81.8
Finland	33	87.9	87.5	78.8	58.8	78.8	78.1	75.8	81.8	75.0	75.0	75.8
France	110	87.3	87.7	87.6	69.2	81.9	81.7	84.3	84.9	84.8	78.5	72.6
Germany	78	84.6	87.2	84.6	76.9	80.3	69.2	75.6	79.2	83.3	77.9	67.9
Greece	28	85.7	79.3	78.6	71.4	82.1	71.4	85.7	80.0	82.8	85.7	65.5
Italy	231	91.8	90.4	91.7	71.1	89.5	89.9	91.2	91.9	90.3	88.0	74.0
Netherlands	53	73.6	75.0	71.2	73.1	71.2	71.2	65.4	67.3	74.5	69.2	67.3
Norway	26	88.5	88.5	88.5	84.0	87.5	73.1	88.0	83.3	84.0	84.0	84.0
Poland	41	90.2	90.0	87.5	72.5	85.4	82.9	85.0	81.6	77.5	80.0	71.8
Portugal	54	94.4	92.9	92.6	81.5	78.2	89.3	90.9	89.1	89.3	83.0	67.3
Romania	26	88.5	92.0	92.0	75.0	84.0	92.0	87.5	88.0	88.0	88.0	76.0
Spain	169	90.5	94.7	91.7	82.1	89.8	89.3	92.1	91.5	90.4	85.1	82.0
Sweden	34	79.4	85.3	85.3	65.6	76.5	71.9	76.5	79.4	79.4	78.8	63.6
Switzerland	25	84.0	84.0	79.2	80.0	80.0	84.0	80.0	84.0	87.5	84.0	72.0
Turkey	40	87.5	84.6	84.6	60.0	79.5	75.0	76.9	77.5	76.9	75.0	56.8
UK & Ireland	131	72.5	73.8	73.6	68.5	70.2	68.8	67.2	68.7	71.3	69.2	65.9
Overall average	**1,338**	**87.1**	**87.3**	**86.3**	**74.0**	**82.6**	**80.9**	**83.3**	**83.7**	**84.1**	**80.5**	**70.6**

Note that the number of respondents per country is only given for the first Standard as there are very slight differences for the other Standards.

When comparing the 21 countries, we notice:

- a high percentage of adequacy for **PA 1000 (Purpose, Authority and Responsibilities)** in Bulgaria, Cyprus, Czech Republic, Italy and Portugal;
- a high percentage of adequacy for **PA 1100 (Independence and Objectivity)** in Bulgaria, Cyprus, Portugal, Romania and Spain;
- a high percentage of adequacy for **PA 1200 (Proficiency and Due Professional Care)** in Bulgaria, Estonia, Portugal, Romania and Spain;

- a high percentage of adequacy for **PA 1300 (Quality Assurance and Improvement Program)** in Bulgaria, Estonia, Norway and Switzerland;
- a high percentage of adequacy for **PA 2000 (Managing the IAA)** in Bulgaria, Estonia, Italy, Spain and Norway;
- a high percentage of adequacy for **PA 2100 (Nature of Work)** in Bulgaria, Estonia, Italy, Romania and Spain;
- a high percentage of adequacy for **PA 2200 (Engagement Planning)** in Bulgaria, Czech Republic, Estonia, Italy and Spain;
- a high percentage of adequacy for **PA 2300 (Performing the Engagement)** in Bulgaria, Estonia, Italy, Portugal and Spain;
- a high percentage of adequacy for **PA 2400 (Communicating Results)** in Bulgaria, Estonia, Italy, Portugal and Spain;
- a high percentage of adequacy for **PA 2500 (Monitoring)** in Bulgaria, Estonia, Greece, Italy and Romania;
- a high percentage of adequacy for **PA 2600 (Management's Acceptance of Risk)** in Bulgaria, Estonia, Norway and Spain.

5.4.   Quality Assessment and Improvement Program

Table 39 shows that AS 1300 on Quality Assurance and Improvement Program (QAIP) has the lowest percentage of compliance. Furthermore, respondents were asked to indicate whether their IA function has a quality assessment and improvement program (QAIP) in accordance with the AS 1300.

Table 41 shows that:

- 29% indicates that there's not a plan to put in place a QAIP in the next twelve months;
- 27% states that their organization currently has a QAIP;
- 22% points out that a QAIP will be put in place within the next twelve months (at the time they completed the questionnaire).

A comparison of the 21 countries shows:

- a high percentage of **QAIP currently in place** in Belgium, Estonia, Romania, Switzerland and UK & Ireland;
- a high percentage of **QAIP in place within the next twelve months** in Bulgaria, Czech Republic, Romania and Switzerland;
- a high percentage of **no plans to put in place a QAIP within the next twelve months** in Cyprus, Greece, Poland, Portugal and Sweden;
- a high percentage of **QAIP not in accordance with Standard 1300** in Austria, Germany and Turkey.

Table 41: Compliance with Standard 1300 (%)

Country	Total Number of respondents	Yes, currently in place	To be put in place within the next twelve months	No plans to put in place in the next twelve months	Your quality assurance program is not in accordance with Standard 1300	I do not know	Total
Austria	77	15.6	15.6	33.8	22.1	13.0	100.0
Belgium	82	40.2	19.5	24.4	11.0	4.9	100.0
Bulgaria	54	14.8	42.6	14.8	13.0	14.8	100.0
Cyprus	27	7.4	25.9	55.6	7.4	3.7	100.0
Czech Republic	151	34.4	21.9	31.8	2.0	9.9	100.0
Estonia	12	58.3	16.7	16.7	8.3	0.0	100.0
Finland	38	34.2	26.3	21.1	7.9	10.5	100.0
France	238	25.2	17.6	34.5	8.0	14.7	100.0
Germany	111	27.0	15.3	27.0	20.7	9.9	100.0
Greece	62	21.0	22.6	40.3	4.8	11.3	100.0
Italy	358	21.2	25.7	31.6	4.2	17.3	100.0
Netherlands	93	31.2	30.1	19.4	8.6	10.8	100.0
Norway	33	24.2	30.3	12.1	15.2	18.2	100.0
Poland	70	10.0	24.3	45.7	7.1	12.9	100.0
Portugal	95	14.7	12.6	40.0	7.4	25.3	100.0
Romania	33	45.5	33.3	3.0	9.1	9.1	100.0
Spain	220	27.7	15.5	31.4	12.7	12.7	100.0
Sweden	43	25.6	20.9	41.9	7.0	4.7	100.0
Switzerland	30	43.3	33.3	3.3	10.0	10.0	100.0
Turkey	61	8.2	23.0	32.8	19.7	16.4	100.0
UK & Ireland	235	45.5	18.3	14.0	7.7	14.5	100.0
Overall average	**2,123**	**27.1**	**21.5**	**28.8**	**9.1**	**13.5**	**100.0**

Table 42 shows that only 23% of the respondents indicate that their internal audit activities have been subject to an internal assessment within the last 12 months and an additional 7% indicate that an assessment has taken place within the last five years. Besides, 42% of the respondents state that their IA function have never had an internal assessment.

Table 42: Compliance with Standard 1311 (%)

Country	Total Number of Respondents	Scheduled to be completed prior to January 1, 2007 but not yet completed	Within the last 12 months	1-3 years ago	4-5 years ago	An internal review more than 5 years ago	Never had an internal assessment	The internal review was not done in accordance with Standard	I don't know	Total
Austria	77	3.9	5.2	3.9	0.0	1.3	54.5	20.8	10.4	100.0
Belgium	82	3.7	32.9	9.8	1.2	0.0	37.8	8.5	6.1	100.0
Bulgaria	53	5.7	9.4	7.5	0.0	0.0	52.8	15.1	9.4	100.0
Cyprus	27	11.1	7.4	7.4	0.0	0.0	59.3	3.7	11.1	100.0
Czech Republic	152	9.9	30.3	2.6	1.3	0.0	50.7	3.3	2.0	100.0
Estonia	13	7.7	38.5	7.7	7.7	0.0	23.1	7.7	7.7	100.0
Finland	39	7.7	17.9	12.8	0.0	0.0	51.3	2.6	7.7	100.0
France	230	3.9	27.4	7.0	0.4	0.0	42.6	17.8	0.9	100.0
Germany	109	0.9	21.1	4.6	0.0	2.8	45.9	12.8	11.9	100.0
Greece	60	5.0	10.0	6.7	0.0	1.7	63.3	1.7	11.7	100.0
Italy	357	10.4	16.8	5.6	0.6	1.1	44.8	19.6	1.1	100.0
Netherlands	93	4.3	35.5	7.5	2.2	0.0	34.4	4.3	11.8	100.0
Norway	32	12.5	28.1	3.1	3.1	0.0	21.9	9.4	21.9	100.0
Poland	71	0.0	29.6	4.2	0.0	0.0	46.5	7.0	12.7	100.0
Portugal	95	2.1	12.6	3.2	1.1	0.0	54.7	5.3	21.1	100.0
Romania	33	15.2	36.4	12.1	0.0	3.0	12.1	12.1	9.1	100.0
Spain	222	6.3	23.0	3.6	1.4	0.9	39.2	14.4	11.3	100.0
Sweden	48	20.8	10.4	6.3	4.2	0.0	27.1	10.4	20.8	100.0
Switzerland	29	6.9	37.9	10.3	0.0	0.0	20.7	13.8	10.3	100.0
Turkey	63	0.0	17.5	6.3	0.0	1.6	65.1	6.3	3.2	100.0
UK & Ireland	235	6.0	33.2	12.8	1.7	2.1	17.4	7.7	19.1	100.0
Overall average	**2,120**	**6.4**	**23.2**	**6.5**	**0.9**	**0.8**	**41.5**	**11.7**	**8.9**	**100.0**

When comparing the 21 countries, we notice:

- a high percentage of **internal assessments scheduled to be completed prior to January 1, 2007 but not yet completed** in Cyprus, Italy, Norway, Romania and Sweden;
- a high percentage of **internal assessments performed within the last 12 months** in Belgium, Estonia, Netherlands, Romania Switzerland and UK & Ireland;
- a high percentage of **internal assessments performed 1-3 years ago** in Finland, Romania, Switzerland and UK & Ireland;
- a high percentage of **internal assessments performed 4-5 years ago** in Estonia, Norway and Sweden;
- a high percentage of **internal assessments performed more than 5 years ago** in Germany, Romania and UK & Ireland;
- a high percentage of **no internal assessments** in Austria, Cyprus, Greece, Portugal and Turkey;
- a high percentage of **internal assessments not done in accordance with Standard 1311** in Austria, France and Italy.

Table 43 shows that only 14% of the respondents indicate that their IA activities have been subject to an external review within the last 12 months. About 11% has been subject to an external review within the last 5 years whereas 47% have never had an external assessment.

Table 43: Compliance with Standard 1312 (%)

Country	Total Number of Respondents	Scheduled to be completed prior to January 1, 2007 but not yet completed	An external review within the last 12 months	1-3 years ago	4-5 years ago	An external review more than 5 years ago	Never had an external assessment	The external review was not done in accordance with Standard	Unsure if a review was performed	Total
Austria	75	2.7	6.7	2.7	1.3	1.3	50.7	24.0	10.7	100.0
Belgium	83	7.2	14.5	18.1	2.4	0.0	39.8	6.0	12.0	100.0
Bulgaria	54	7.4	11.1	3.7	0.0	0.0	59.3	13.0	5.6	100.0
Cyprus	26	3.8	3.8	0.0	0.0	0.0	73.1	11.5	7.7	100.0
Czech Republic	153	9.8	12.4	9.8	0.7	0.0	61.4	2.0	3.9	100.0
Estonia	13	23.1	15.4	0.0	7.7	0.0	30.8	15.4	7.7	100.0
Finland	39	15.4	7.7	15.4	0.0	0.0	48.7	5.1	7.7	100.0
France	228	5.7	18.4	9.2	1.3	0.0	34.2	18.0	13.2	100.0
Germany	110	4.5	10.9	7.3	1.8	0.9	48.2	13.6	12.7	100.0
Greece	60	8.3	11.7	13.3	0.0	1.7	48.3	1.7	15.0	100.0
Italy	355	7.9	9.3	4.5	0.8	0.0	55.5	5.1	16.9	100.0
Netherlands	93	9.7	17.2	9.7	1.1	0.0	44.1	5.4	12.9	100.0
Norway	32	18.8	12.5	9.4	3.1	0.0	40.6	0.0	15.6	100.0
Poland	71	4.2	7.0	19.7	0.0	0.0	50.7	7.0	11.3	100.0
Portugal	95	0.0	8.4	5.3	0.0	1.1	55.8	4.2	25.3	100.0
Romania	32	12.5	31.3	12.5	3.1	0.0	28.1	9.4	3.1	100.0
Spain	223	2.7	12.6	5.8	0.4	0.9	57.8	6.3	13.5	100.0
Sweden	48	16.7	16.7	2.1	6.3	2.1	33.3	12.5	10.4	100.0
Switzerland	30	3.3	16.7	6.7	23.3	10.0	26.7	6.7	6.7	100.0
Turkey	62	1.6	11.3	8.1	0.0	0.0	74.2	0.0	4.8	100.0
UK & Ireland	234	4.7	22.6	22.2	2.6	3.0	20.1	6.0	18.8	100.0
Overall average	**2,116**	**6.5**	**13.5**	**9.5**	**1.6**	**0.8**	**47.0**	**7.9**	**13.2**	**100.0**

Comparing the results between all 21 countries reveals:

- a high percentage of **external reviews scheduled to be completed prior to January 1, 2007 but not yet completed** in Estonia, Finland, Norway, Romania and Sweden;
- a high percentage of **external reviews completed within the last twelve months** in France, Netherlands, Romania and UK & Ireland;
- a high percentage of **external reviews completed 1-3 years ago** in Belgium, Finland, Poland and UK & Ireland;
- a high percentage of **external reviews completed 4-5 years ago** in Estonia, Sweden and Switzerland;
- a high percentage of **external reviews completed more than 5 years ago** in Sweden, Switzerland and UK & Ireland;
- a high percentage of **no external reviews** in Bulgaria, Cyprus, Czech Republic, Spain and Turkey;
- a high percentage of **external reviews not done in accordance with Standard** in Austria, Bulgaria, Estonia and France.

According to Table 44, the most commons activities performed as part of the QAIP are:

- Engagement supervision (41%);
- Use of checklists / manuals to provide assurance that proper audit processes are followed (38%);
- Feedback of the audit customer at the end of an audit (36%).

Comparing the 21 countries reveals:

- a high percentage of **verification that the IA function is in compliance with the IIA Standards** as part of the QAIP in Belgium, Czech Republic, Estonia and Switzerland;
- a high percentage of **compliance with non-IIA standards or codes** as part of the QAIP in Netherlands, Poland, Switzerland and UK & Ireland;
- a high percentage of **Internal Audit professionals are in compliance with The IIA Code of Ethics** as part of the QAIP in Czech Republic, Estonia, Finland, Poland and Switzerland;
- a high percentage of **checklists / manuals to provide assurance** as part of the QAIP in Belgium, Estonia, Netherlands, Switzerland and UK & Ireland;
- a high percentage of **engagement supervision** as part of the QAIP in Belgium, Germany, Spain, Switzerland and UK & Ireland;
- a high percentage of **feedback from audit customers** as part of the QAIP in Belgium, Czech Republic, Estonia, Netherlands and UK & Ireland;
- a high percentage of **reviews by other members of the internal audit function** as part of the QAIP in Belgium, Netherlands, Norway, Spain and UK & Ireland;
- a high percentage of **reviews by external party** as part of the QAIP in Estonia, Germany, Netherlands, Switzerland and UK & Ireland.

Table 44: Activities as Part of your Quality Assessment and Improvement Program (%)

Country	Total Number of Respondents	Verification that the IA Function is in compliance with The IIA Standards	Compliance with non-IIA standards or codes	Internal audit professionals are in compliance with The IIA Code of Ethics	Checklists / manuals to provide assurance	Engagement supervision	Feedback from audit customers at the end of an audit	Reviews by other members of the internal audit function	Review by external party	I do not know	Not applicable
Austria	88	14.8	9.1	26.1	45.5	42.0	22.7	12.5	25.0	4.5	12.5
Belgium	94	39.4	18.1	31.9	48.9	53.2	51.1	40.4	18.1	4.3	11.7
Bulgaria	84	21.4	11.9	31.0	38.1	17.9	21.4	13.1	15.5	3.6	7.1
Cyprus	29	20.7	13.8	34.5	44.8	31.0	24.1	17.2	13.8	10.3	24.1
Czech Republic	175	38.9	14.9	37.7	28.0	20.6	50.9	22.3	13.1	5.1	14.9
Estonia	14	50.0	14.3	50.0	57.1	42.9	64.3	14.3	28.6	7.1	7.1
Finland	42	35.7	9.5	42.9	42.9	40.5	50.0	33.3	16.7	7.1	14.3
France	259	28.6	16.6	27.8	34.7	51.4	34.4	28.6	15.8	7.7	13.9
Germany	134	20.9	12.7	31.3	48.5	53.7	37.3	20.9	26.1	3.0	12.7
Greece	73	16.4	11.0	17.8	37.0	35.6	27.4	21.9	13.7	4.1	17.8
Italy	447	21.7	10.5	22.4	23.9	24.6	18.3	13.9	9.4	12.8	22.4
Netherlands	101	31.7	31.7	24.8	62.4	50.5	55.4	51.5	37.6	6.9	8.9
Norway	42	35.7	16.7	28.6	40.5	35.7	35.7	42.9	21.4	7.1	4.8
Poland	88	30.7	33.0	51.1	30.7	44.3	37.5	27.3	10.2	4.5	5.7
Portugal	125	16.0	10.4	22.4	28.0	40.0	30.4	22.4	10.4	10.4	14.4
Romania	69	24.6	18.8	24.6	30.4	31.9	29.0	20.3	18.8	0.0	4.3
Spain	242	24.0	22.7	38.8	40.1	64.0	43.0	35.1	13.6	6.2	12.4
Sweden	59	30.5	13.6	30.5	28.8	33.9	33.9	18.6	16.9	13.6	10.2
Switzerland	33	48.5	30.3	51.5	63.6	72.7	48.5	24.2	33.3	0.0	6.1
Turkey	80	16.3	12.5	23.8	27.5	36.3	25.0	28.8	8.8	2.5	23.8
UK & Ireland	259	27.0	31.3	26.6	54.1	51.7	55.2	45.2	34.4	9.7	5.0
Overall average	**2,537**	**26.1**	**17.5**	**29.6**	**37.6**	**41.4**	**36.2**	**26.8**	**17.7**	**7.4**	**13.4**

Note that percentages do not add up to 100% as respondents could mark all that apply.

6 Internal Audit Activities

In the sixth section of the questionnaire, all respondents had to indicate the activities performed by their internal audit function followed by the evolution in internal audit activities. Next, all respondents were asked to indicate when major differences around audit issues are resolved as well as who has primary responsibility for reporting to senior management and monitoring corrective action.

6.1. Internal Audit Activities

According to Table 45, the four most common internal audit activities are:

- Operational audits (80%)
- Internal control testing and systems evaluation (78%)
- Control framework monitoring and development (62%)
- Investigations of fraud and irregularities (61%)

When comparing all 21 European countries. we notice:

- a high percentage of **business viability assessments** in Austria, Germany, Norway, Sweden, Switzerland and Turkey;
- a high percentage of **compliance with privacy polices audits** in Belgium, Cyprus, Greece, Netherlands, Norway and Switzerland;
- a high percentage of **compliance with corporate governance requirements audits** in Belgium, Greece, Netherlands, Norway, Switzerland and UK & Ireland;
- a high percentage of **control framework monitoring and development** in Austria, Finland, Germany, Netherlands and Switzerland;
- a high percentage of involvement in **corporate takeovers and mergers** in Belgium, Greece, Netherlands, Spain and Switzerland;
- a high percentage of involvement in **enterprise risk management** in Estonia, France, Norway and Switzerland;
- a high percentage of **ethics audits** in Belgium, Cyprus, Czech Republic, Estonia and Norway;
- a high percentage of **external audit assistance** in Austria, Estonia, Portugal, Spain and Switzerland;
- a high percentage of **health, safety and environment audits** in Cyprus, Estonia, Finland, France and UK & Ireland;
- a high percentage of **financial auditing** in Austria, Cyprus, Germany, Switzerland and UK & Ireland;
- a high percentage of **information risk assessments** in Germany, Sweden and Switzerland;
- a high percentage of **information technology department assessments** in Belgium, Germany, Sweden, Switzerland and UK & Ireland;
- a high percentage of **internal control testing / systems evaluations** in Belgium, Cyprus, Netherlands, Switzerland and UK & Ireland;

- a high percentage of **investigations of fraud and irregularities** in Austria, Cyprus, Germany, Spain and Switzerland;
- a high percentage of **linkage of company strategy and company performance** in Austria, Estonia, Finland, Norway and Switzerland;
- a high percentage of **management effectiveness audits** in Belgium, Czech Republic, Norway, Sweden and UK & Ireland;
- a high percentage of **operational audits** in Belgium, Norway, Sweden and UK & Ireland,
- a high percentage of **quality / ISO audits** in Cyprus, Finland, France, Norway and Spain;
- a high percentage of involvement in **resource management and controls** in Austria, Estonia, Finland, Sweden and UK & Ireland;
- a high percentage of involvement in **security issues** in Austria, Belgium, Cyprus, Finland, Germany and UK & Ireland;
- a high percentage of **social and sustainability audits** in Austria, Germany and Norway;
- a high percentage of **special projects** in Austria, Cyprus, Finland, Germany, Netherlands, Switzerland and UK & Ireland;
- a high percentage of involvement in **technical competency training for auditors** in Belgium, Portugal, Switzerland and UK & Ireland.

Table 45: Activities Performed by the Internal Audit Function (%)

Country	Total Number of Respondents	Business Viability Assessments	Compliance with Privacy Policies	Compliance with Corporate Governance Requirements	Control Framework Monitoring and Development	Corporate Takeovers / Mergers	Enterprise Risk Management	Ethics Audits	External Audit Assistance	Health, Safety and Environment	Financial Auditing	Information Risk Assessment
Austria	83	50.6	42.2	41.0	71.1	4.8	32.5	18.1	63.9	18.1	72.3	54.2
Belgium	92	27.2	52.2	64.1	59.8	13.0	42.4	55.4	44.6	19.6	58.7	51.1
Bulgaria	80	16.3	23.8	36.3	48.8	5.0	35.0	27.5	13.8	15.0	41.3	38.8
Cyprus	27	14.8	63.0	51.9	63.0	7.4	37.0	59.3	37.0	25.9	70.4	29.6
Czech Republic	174	10.3	23.6	33.9	56.9	3.4	38.5	74.1	45.4	11.5	59.2	48.9
Estonia	14	14.3	50.0	42.9	50.0	0.0	57.1	64.3	57.1	28.6	35.7	57.1
Finland	42	26.2	50.0	59.5	73.8	9.5	35.7	47.6	40.5	23.8	52.4	57.1
France	252	19.4	36.1	48.8	52.4	7.5	48.4	43.7	20.6	23.8	52.0	44.0
Germany	127	43.4	42.5	49.6	74.0	10.2	34.6	25.2	51.2	13.4	71.7	66.1
Greece	73	27.4	58.9	64.4	61.6	16.4	27.4	38.4	13.7	17.8	47.9	28.8
Italy	440	13.6	46.6	59.8	69.8	11.8	43.2	51.1	42.0	20.2	62.0	53.0
Netherlands	99	22.2	54.5	76.8	70.7	14.1	39.4	41.4	51.5	19.2	56.6	53.5
Norway	36	36.1	66.7	80.6	52.8	8.3	55.6	63.9	38.9	19.4	33.3	44.4
Poland	86	22.1	30.2	48.8	64.0	3.5	29.1	32.6	40.7	15.1	52.3	54.7
Portugal	119	9.2	34.5	35.3	39.5	5.0	22.7	29.4	52.9	19.3	41.2	40.3
Romania	64	10.9	25.0	28.1	26.6	4.7	28.1	37.5	4.7	7.8	12.5	26.6
Spain	238	16.4	37.4	45.8	69.7	16.4	39.5	36.6	55.0	16.0	51.3	50.8
Sweden	58	65.5	41.4	50.0	50.0	10.3	25.9	44.8	48.3	20.7	56.9	58.6
Switzerland	32	43.8	56.3	71.9	84.4	21.9	50.0	37.5	75.0	15.6	75.0	68.8
Turkey	77	37.7	40.3	41.6	50.6	9.1	23.4	45.5	22.1	15.6	51.9	46.8
UK & Ireland	253	23.3	36.8	67.2	70.4	7.5	37.2	37.9	43.9	26.5	75.5	54.5
Overall Average	2,466	22.3	40.4	52.4	62.1	9.5	38.0	43.1	40.9	18.9	57.0	49.8

Country	Information Technology Department Assessment	Internal Control Systems / Testing / Evaluation	Investigations of Fraud and Irregularities	Linkage of Strategy and Company Performance	Management Effectiveness Audit	Operational Audits	Quality / ISO Audits	Resource Management and Controls	Security Issues	Social and Sustainability Audits	Special Projects	Technical Competency Training for Auditors
Austria	49.4	80.7	74.7	38.6	24.1	69.9	2.4	44.6	50.6	45.8	47.0	14.5
Belgium	55.4	90.2	52.2	35.9	62.0	92.4	19.6	25.0	46.7	20.7	44.6	50.0
Bulgaria	30.0	53.8	40.0	16.3	35.0	62.5	10.0	28.8	21.3	16.3	15.0	18.8
Cyprus	29.6	88.9	81.5	22.2	44.4	85.2	22.2	25.9	48.1	11.1	51.9	44.4
Czech Republic	34.5	81.6	44.3	32.8	63.2	73.6	13.8	20.7	20.7	10.9	14.4	14.9
Estonia	28.6	78.6	57.1	50.0	57.1	78.6	7.1	50.0	28.6	21.4	35.7	14.3
Finland	52.4	73.8	57.1	47.6	54.8	81.0	21.4	50.0	54.8	23.8	47.6	35.7
France	42.5	77.8	59.5	14.3	51.6	75.4	21.0	29.0	35.3	26.6	31.0	35.7
Germany	65.4	77.2	75.6	29.9	26.0	80.3	5.5	31.5	47.2	33.1	59.1	33.1
Greece	35.6	74.0	68.5	21.9	42.5	78.1	8.2	24.7	32.9	19.2	42.5	35.6
Italy	41.8	72.0	58.9	22.0	40.5	80.5	10.5	18.0	27.7	11.8	32.0	47.5
Netherlands	51.5	89.9	66.7	29.3	44.4	88.9	16.2	20.2	41.4	19.2	60.6	47.5
Norway	47.2	77.8	69.4	41.7	63.9	91.7	27.8	27.8	41.7	30.6	36.1	44.4
Poland	47.7	75.6	25.6	24.4	58.1	79.1	8.1	38.4	41.9	25.6	18.6	46.5
Portugal	39.5	79.0	67.2	21.8	45.4	74.8	19.3	20.2	27.7	20.2	30.3	52.1
Romania	20.3	42.2	20.3	18.8	31.3	42.2	10.9	18.8	14.1	10.9	10.9	25.0
Spain	37.8	84.5	76.5	24.4	34.0	84.9	23.9	31.9	31.5	15.1	38.7	45.8
Sweden	69.0	74.1	63.8	37.9	63.8	91.4	15.5	43.1	34.5	19.0	34.5	37.9
Switzerland	71.9	96.9	87.5	40.6	34.4	96.9	15.6	40.6	43.8	15.6	65.6	50.0
Turkey	39.0	59.7	64.9	22.1	29.9	68.8	6.5	28.6	22.1	23.4	22.1	32.5
UK & Ireland	58.9	90.5	68.4	34.0	60.9	89.3	17.0	42.3	46.2	26.1	58.1	49.4
Overall Average	45.1	77.8	61.0	26.5	45.7	79.6	14.7	28.6	34.5	20.2	36.9	39.5

6.2.   Evolution of Internal Audit Activities

When studying the overall evolutions in the period 2003-2009, Table 46 shows an increase in the importance of consulting / advisory, governance audits, information technology audits and management audits. On the contrary, we notice a decrease in the importance of compliance audits, financial process audits and operational audits. The proportion of fraud investigations remains stable over this 6 years period.

When comparing the 21 European countries, we notice:

- a strong decrease in the proportion of **compliance audits** in Estonia and Poland and Romania;
- a strong increase in the proportion of **consulting / advisory** in Cyprus, Estonia and Romania;
- a strong decrease in the proportion of **financial process audits** in Greece, Netherlands and UK & Ireland;
- a strong increase in the proportion of **governance audits** in Finland, Netherlands, Norway, Portugal, Romania, Spain and UK & Ireland;
- a strong increase in the proportion of **information technology audits** in Estonia, Romania and Turkey;
- a strong decrease in the proportion of **operational audits** in Estonia, Spain and UK & Ireland;
- a strong increase in the proportion of **management audits** in Estonia;

Table 46: Evolution of Internal Audit Activities (%)

Country	Compliance Audits			Consulting / Advisory			Financial Process Audits			Fraud Investigations		
	3 Years Ago	Currently (2006)	3 Years from Now	3 Years Ago	Currently (2006)	3 Years from Now	3 Years Ago	Currently (2006)	3 Years from Now	3 Years Ago	Currently (2006)	3 Years from Now
Austria	26.0	26.0	22.6	10.0	11.8	12.6	11.1	10.0	9.1	7.6	8.3	9.3
Belgium	17.2	17.3	15.7	9.1	12.3	12.4	10.7	11.7	11.6	5.1	3.8	4.5
Bulgaria	23.6	21.6	17.4	7.0	11.6	10.5	10.7	11.5	11.0	7.8	7.1	9.0
Cyprus	26.3	20.0	19.0	5.7	11.8	17.5	13.4	14.4	12.1	4.2	4.7	3.8
Czech Republic	26.5	25.4	21.4	9.6	13.0	16.7	15.6	12.3	13.8	4.0	3.7	4.1
Estonia	30.9	22.3	8.4	8.8	19.8	17.1	6.4	6.7	7.5	6.1	3.8	4.2
Finland	16.7	14.8	12.2	15.2	14.7	17.9	16.7	12.5	11.8	5.2	4.3	5.5
France	22.8	22.7	19.2	8.6	9.3	10.7	13.6	12.7	13.2	4.6	4.7	5.6
Germany	25.5	21.4	18.0	9.6	15.7	16.6	13.6	11.3	10.6	4.9	6.4	7.5
Greece	12.6	15.9	15.2	10.3	12.9	16.3	19.9	18.0	13.7	9.1	8.2	7.2
Italy	28.1	26.8	24.7	6.6	10.2	12.1	14.1	12.9	12.8	5.8	4.5	4.8
Netherlands	12.9	17.1	16.5	8.5	8.3	8.5	29.6	21.3	18.3	2.6	2.8	3.0
Norway	14.1	26.3	16.6	13.2	8.6	8.0	9.9	7.5	6.9	3.9	5.8	4.5
Poland	31.0	29.7	22.9	6.9	10.8	14.8	11.7	16.7	11.9	2.0	2.3	2.7
Portugal	24.0	17.9	16.3	6.6	9.6	9.3	12.8	11.0	11.6	5.7	6.4	6.0
Romania	56.8	32.4	21.9	3.1	13.3	16.2	5.7	8.7	8.6	5.0	4.0	5.6
Spain	20.2	18.9	17.0	7.6	10.2	10.8	16.9	14.6	12.6	6.8	5.7	6.4
Sweden	22.5	17.8	14.9	8.1	7.9	11.1	10.6	14.3	11.8	3.5	3.2	3.1
Switzerland	19.7	17.2	17.7	7.9	7.1	9.1	20.6	18.8	16.8	4.7	4.4	4.8
Turkey	28.3	26.7	24.7	9.8	9.6	15.6	13.4	15.4	12.9	13.0	11.0	12.0
UK & Ireland	14.3	12.8	11.9	8.1	10.0	12.3	20.6	17.5	14.5	5.1	5.0	4.8
Overall Average	22.6	21.2	18.5	8.3	10.8	12.3	15.4	13.7	12.8	5.4	5.1	5.5

Country	Governance			Information Technology Audits			Operational Audits			Management Audits		
	3 Years Ago	Currently (2006)	3 Years from Now	3 Years Ago	Currently (2006)	3 Years from Now	3 Years Ago	Currently (2006)	3 Years from Now	3 Years Ago	Currently (2006)	3 Years from Now
Austria	9.5	10.9	11.1	5.5	7.8	7.8	14.1	14.8	17.1	2.3	2.8	3.9
Belgium	4.4	5.9	7.7	8.9	10.9	12.1	30.6	28.9	24.5	7.3	6.8	7.7
Bulgaria	3.5	5.2	6.7	4.6	5.0	9.7	23.6	26.1	18.9	7.1	6.2	7.7
Cyprus	3.4	4.0	6.5	2.9	4.5	7.2	26.7	25.5	21.3	2.7	5.6	4.8
Czech Republic	5.3	7.1	8.5	6.4	8.2	10.5	19.6	17.8	15.6	5.6	8.6	7.5
Estonia	4.1	5.3	5.8	3.9	10.3	21.8	25.0	19.1	18.3	6.0	7.1	10.0
Finland	5.1	10.6	10.6	7.6	9.9	12.7	21.7	23.2	20.0	8.8	5.9	6.4
France	4.7	6.4	7.1	6.8	8.0	9.8	21.9	20.2	20.7	11.0	10.2	9.6
Germany	6.6	9.0	9.4	11.2	12.0	13.9	17.2	18.1	18.9	1.8	2.3	3.3
Greece	5.5	6.4	8.4	4.3	4.3	9.0	23.6	26.1	19.9	4.0	4.5	4.9
Italy	6.1	9.7	10.8	5.6	5.9	7.2	25.5	22.1	21.8	1.5	2.1	2.6
Netherlands	2.8	5.9	7.8	11.1	12.1	12.8	26.1	26.5	27.1	1.7	3.0	3.4
Norway	5.5	9.7	10.0	7.1	11.1	12.7	35.0	34.7	33.0	3.6	5.0	5.9
Poland	3.6	6.1	6.9	4.2	7.4	10.4	20.2	20.3	18.4	7.8	6.6	8.7
Portugal	1.4	3.0	6.9	7.7	10.0	13.2	30.5	31.6	27.4	7.9	6.6	7.3
Romania	5.7	8.2	11.2	2.2	7.1	10.2	8.4	16.2	12.9	3.9	3.7	6.4
Spain	3.4	5.6	9.0	4.1	6.5	9.9	25.3	23.5	20.0	10.6	12.3	11.7
Sweden	9.8	10.0	11.8	9.2	11.2	13.6	24.9	23.4	22.2	3.2	5.1	6.1
Switzerland	6.2	8.9	6.7	11.4	12.1	13.4	21.2	21.6	20.2	3.8	5.6	5.6
Turkey	4.6	4.6	6.6	3.0	5.4	9.4	19.6	21.2	15.7	3.7	3.9	4.1
UK & Ireland	5.5	8.7	11.1	9.5	10.7	12.7	28.7	26.4	23.5	5.0	6.5	6.8
Overall Average	**5.1**	**7.4**	**9.1**	**6.9**	**8.3**	**10.7**	**23.8**	**22.9**	**21.1**	**5.5**	**6.2**	**6.5**

6.3.   Resolving Major Differences around Audit Issues

In general, major differences around audit issues are usually revolved during the fieldwork and audit reporting, but rarely during planning and after the audit report is issued (cf. Table 47).

Table 47: Resolving Major Differences around Audit Issues

Country	During Planning	During Audit Fieldwork	During Audit Reporting	After Audit Report is Issued	Never
Austria	Never	Usually	Usually	Rarely	Never
Belgium	Rarely	Usually	Usually	Rarely	Never
Bulgaria	Rarely / Usually	Usually	Sometimes	Usually	Never
Cyprus	Rarely / Sometimes	Sometimes/ Usually	Usually	Sometimes / Usually	Never
Czech Republic	Sometimes	Usually	Usually	Rarely	Never
Estonia	Usually	Usually	Usually	Usually / Always	Never
Finland	Sometimes	Sometimes	Usually	Rarely	Never
France	Rarely	Usually	Usually	Rarely	Never
Germany	Never	Usually	Usually	Rarely	Never
Greece	Sometimes	Usually	Usually	Usually	Never
Italy	Rarely	Usually	Usually	Rarely	Never
Netherlands	Sometimes	Usually	Usually	Rarely	Never
Norway	Rarely	Sometimes	Usually	Rarely	Never
Poland	Rarely	Sometimes	Usually	Usually	Never
Portugal	Rarely	Sometimes	Usually	Rarely	Never
Romania	Never/ Sometimes	Usually	Sometimes	Never	Never
Spain	Rarely	Sometimes	Usually	Rarely	Never
Sweden	Sometimes	Sometimes	Usually	Rarely	Never
Switzerland	Rarely	Sometimes	Usually	Rarely	Never
Turkey	Sometimes	Usually	Usually	Rarely	Never
UK & Ireland	Sometimes	Sometimes	Usually	Rarely	Never
Overall Average	**Rarely**	**Usually**	**Usually**	**Rarely**	**Never**

Note that for each category the response with the highest frequency is shown. Respondents could indicate: never, rarely, sometimes, usually or always.

A comparison of the 21 European countries reveals that:

- major differences around audit issues are usually resolved **during planning** in Bulgaria and Estonia;
- major differences around audit issues are usually resolved **after the audit report is issued** in Bulgaria, Cyprus, Estonia, Greece and Poland.

6.4. Reporting and Follow-up of Audit Results

Overall, Table 48 shows that in a majority of the cases, the CAE is primarily responsible for reporting audit results to senior management.

Table 48: Primary Responsibility for Reporting of Audit Results (%)

Country	Total Number of Respondents	Auditee / Client	CAE	Internal Audit Manager	Both Internal Audit Manager and Auditee	Both CAE and Auditee	Other	No Formal Reporting of Results	Total
Austria	74	4.1	75.7	9.5	2.7	5.4	0.0	2.7	100.0
Belgium	82	1.2	51.2	34.1	6.1	3.7	1.2	2.4	100.0
Bulgaria	53	1.9	49.1	32.1	1.9	11.3	1.9	1.9	100.0
Cyprus	26	0.0	53.8	42.3	0.0	3.8	0.0	0.0	100.0
Czech Republic	146	0.7	84.9	11.0	0.7	0.7	2.1	0.0	100.0
Estonia	13	0.0	53.8	30.8	0.0	7.7	7.7	0.0	100.0
Finland	38	0.0	60.5	31.6	7.9	0.0	0.0	0.0	100.0
France	215	0.5	65.1	27.9	3.3	1.4	0.9	0.9	100.0
Germany	102	1.0	68.6	15.7	7.8	5.9	1.0	0.0	100.0
Greece	63	3.2	47.6	38.1	3.2	6.3	1.6	0.0	100.0
Italy	377	4.2	74.5	11.9	2.1	3.7	0.5	2.9	100.0
Netherlands	94	4.3	37.2	31.9	13.8	12.8	0.0	0.0	100.0
Norway	34	8.8	44.1	17.6	14.7	5.9	5.9	2.9	100.0
Poland	69	1.4	71.0	8.7	1.4	14.5	1.4	1.4	100.0
Portugal	97	2.1	59.8	26.8	3.1	5.2	1.0	2.1	100.0
Romania	28	0.0	60.7	28.6	3.6	0.0	3.6	3.6	100.0
Spain	221	1.4	70.1	14.0	3.6	8.6	0.5	1.8	100.0
Sweden	55	9.1	49.1	25.5	10.9	3.6	1.8	0.0	100.0
Switzerland	31	0.0	77.4	12.9	3.2	6.5	0.0	0.0	100.0
Turkey	61	1.6	67.2	23.0	1.6	3.3	1.6	1.6	100.0
UK & Ireland	234	3.4	43.6	28.2	16.7	4.7	3.0	0.4	100.0
Overall Average	**2,113**	**2.5**	**63.2**	**21.1**	**5.4**	**5.1**	**1.3**	**1.4**	**100.0**

When comparing all 21 European countries we see

- a high percentage of **auditees primarily responsible for reporting of audit results to senior management** in Norway and Swede;
- a high percentage of **CAEs primarily responsible for reporting of audit results to senior management** in Austria, Czech Republic, Italy and Switzerland;

- a high percentage of **audit managers primarily responsible for reporting of audit results to senior management** in Belgium, Bulgaria, Cyprus, Finland and Greece;
- a high percentage of both **audit managers and auditees primarily responsible for reporting of audit results to senior management** in Netherlands, Norway, Sweden and UK & Ireland;
- a high percentage of **CAEs and auditees primarily responsible for reporting of audit results to senior management** in Bulgaria, Netherlands and Poland;
- a high percentage of **other parties primarily responsible for reporting of audit results to senior management** in Estonia and Norway;
- a high percentage of **no reporting of audit results to senior management** in Italy, Norway and Romania.

Table 49: Primary Responsibility for Monitoring Corrective Action (%)

Country	Total Number of Respondents	Auditee / Client	Internal Auditor	Both Internal Auditor and Auditee	Other	No Formal Follow-up	Total
Austria	74	13.5	29.7	54.1	0.0	2.7	100.0
Belgium	82	8.5	32.9	57.3	0.0	1.2	100.0
Bulgaria	53	7.5	39.6	47.2	1.9	3.8	100.0
Cyprus	26	15.4	23.1	50.0	0.0	11.5	100.0
Czech Republic	146	12.3	45.9	39.7	0.0	2.1	100.0
Estonia	13	0.0	23.1	61.5	15.4	0.0	100.0
Finland	38	28.9	23.7	44.7	0.0	2.6	100.0
France	216	6.0	39.8	50.5	0.9	2.8	100.0
Germany	103	14.6	26.2	55.3	2.9	1.0	100.0
Greece	61	9.8	45.9	36.1	1.6	6.6	100.0
Italy	376	12.0	36.7	45.2	1.3	4.8	100.0
Netherlands	95	31.6	15.8	48.4	0.0	4.2	100.0
Norway	34	32.4	2.9	58.8	5.9	0.0	100.0
Poland	70	11.4	30.0	47.1	1.4	10.0	100.0
Portugal	97	3.1	42.3	48.5	3.1	3.1	100.0
Romania	28	21.4	53.6	21.4	0.0	3.6	100.0
Spain	221	10.0	47.1	38.9	0.9	3.2	100.0
Sweden	54	31.5	5.6	61.1	1.9	0.0	100.0
Switzerland	32	18.8	21.9	50.0	9.4	0.0	100.0
Turkey	61	11.5	32.8	42.6	0.0	13.1	100.0
UK & Ireland	234	16.7	29.1	52.1	1.3	0.9	100.0
Overall Average	**2,114**	**13.3**	**34.5**	**47.4**	**1.4**	**3.5**	**100.0**

In almost half of the cases (47%), the primary responsibility for monitoring corrective action lies with both the internal auditor and the auditee, whereas in 35% of the cases, this responsibility only lies with the internal auditor (cf. Table 49).

Comparing all 21 European countries reveals:

- a high percentage of **auditees primarily responsible for monitoring corrective action** in Finland, Netherlands, Norway and Sweden;
- a high percentage of **internal auditors primarily responsible for monitoring corrective action** in Czech Republic, Greece, Romania and Spain;
- a high percentage of **both internal auditors and auditees primarily responsible for monitoring corrective action** in Belgium, Estonia, Norway and Sweden;
- a high percentage of **other parties primarily responsible for monitoring corrective action** in Estonia, Norway, Portugal and Switzerland;
- a high percentage of no monitoring of corrective action in Cyprus, Poland and Turkey.

7 Tools, Skills and Competencies

In the seventh section of the questionnaire, all respondents had to indicate how intensively they currently use specific internal audit tools as well as how important they consider some specific knowledge areas (not completed by CAEs). Besides, CAEs had to mark the five most important behavioural skills, technical skills and competences for each hierarchical level in the internal audit function.

7.1. Internal Audit Tools

Table 50: Current Use of Internal Audit Tools (means)

Country	Analytical review	Balanced scorecard or similar framework	Benchmarking	Computer Assisted Audit Techniques	Continuous / real-time auditing	Control Self Assessment	Data mining	Electronic work papers
Austria	3.26	1.56	2.36	2.94	2.74	1.62	1.92	2.48
Belgium	3.28	2.11	2.26	2.60	1.79	2.37	2.48	3.49
Bulgaria	3.44	1.64	2.59	2.29	2.56	2.26	2.51	2.92
Cyprus	3.46	1.60	2.29	1.71	2.21	1.71	2.18	2.58
Czech Republic	3.78	1.94	2.44	2.36	2.50	2.53	2.59	3.72
Estonia	3.10	1.56	2.50	2.10	2.10	2.90	2.38	3.50
Finland	3.14	2.51	2.69	2.58	2.28	2.34	2.08	3.14
France	2.91	2.45	2.46	2.44	1.78	2.31	3.28	3.55
Germany	3.48	1.66	2.34	2.88	2.60	1.87	2.04	3.00
Greece	3.43	1.91	2.44	2.70	2.84	2.12	2.88	3.53
Italy	3.02	1.77	2.20	2.25	2.02	2.35	1.87	3.76
Netherlands	3.28	1.92	2.18	2.52	1.95	2.48	2.09	3.22
Norway	3.03	2.00	2.37	2.20	1.72	1.97	1.80	3.67
Poland	3.03	1.61	1.72	2.24	2.30	2.55	3.14	3.08
Portugal	3.02	1.64	2.10	2.73	2.40	2.12	1.73	3.40
Romania	3.46	2.37	2.48	2.04	2.54	2.44	2.54	3.15
Spain	3.41	2.68	2.23	2.68	2.49	2.35	2.10	3.20
Sweden	3.40	1.88	2.60	2.27	1.86	2.23	1.59	3.10
Switzerland	3.25	1.53	2.41	2.75	2.39	1.97	2.47	3.13
Turkey	3.83	1.91	2.91	3.18	2.84	2.66	3.12	3.39
UK & Ireland	2.84	1.88	2.28	2.45	1.93	2.26	1.88	3.26
Overall Average	**3.21**	**1.99**	**2.32**	**2.50**	**2.21**	**2.28**	**2.29**	**3.36**

1 = Not Used, 2 = Moderately Used, 3 = Average Use,
4 = Very Much Used, 5 = Extensively Used

Country	Flowchart software	Other electronic communication (e.g. Internet, email)	Process mapping application	Process modeling software	Risk based audit planning	Statistical sampling	The IIA's Quality Assessment Review tools	Total quality management techniques
Austria	1.79	3.96	2.08	1.77	3.28	2.66	1.63	1.50
Belgium	2.31	4.13	2.38	1.61	3.69	2.46	2.17	1.90
Bulgaria	2.20	3.51	2.65	1.50	3.02	2.04	1.81	1.98
Cyprus	2.13	3.88	2.50	1.50	2.96	2.22	1.67	1.83
Czech Republic	2.42	4.32	2.26	1.64	3.78	2.93	2.42	2.16
Estonia	2.78	4.50	2.50	1.20	4.20	2.20	2.30	1.80
Finland	2.19	4.25	1.94	1.60	3.64	2.44	2.33	2.00
France	2.09	4.17	2.61	1.72	3.36	2.52	1.65	1.70
Germany	2.27	4.26	2.38	1.81	3.91	2.67	1.96	1.87
Greece	2.30	4.24	2.54	1.87	3.20	2.61	1.77	1.96
Italy	2.60	3.80	2.79	1.86	3.31	2.83	1.86	1.57
Netherlands	2.15	4.13	2.07	1.62	3.67	2.35	1.89	1.98
Norway	1.90	4.07	1.97	1.70	3.87	2.03	1.90	1.72
Poland	2.33	4.17	1.97	1.69	3.88	2.90	1.39	1.57
Portugal	2.46	4.01	2.49	1.67	3.22	3.10	1.53	1.70
Romania	2.44	3.71	2.11	1.96	3.89	2.68	1.96	1.92
Spain	2.22	3.96	2.68	1.85	3.46	3.00	1.86	1.64
Sweden	2.04	4.66	1.73	1.38	4.00	1.91	1.72	1.42
Switzerland	2.56	3.97	2.53	2.06	4.03	2.63	2.44	1.97
Turkey	2.48	4.18	2.25	1.78	3.21	3.04	1.66	2.04
UK & Ireland	1.96	4.22	1.97	1.36	3.90	2.56	1.62	1.75
Overall average	**2.27**	**4.08**	**2.40**	**1.70**	**3.54**	**2.68**	**1.84**	**1.76**

1 = Not Used, 2 = Moderately Used, 3 = Average Use,
4 = Very Much Used, 5 = Extensively Used

Table 50 shows that the following audit tools are currently most extensively used:

- Other electronic communication (e.g., Internet, email) (average score of 4.08)
- Risk based audit planning (average score of 3.54)
- Electronic work papers (average score of 3.36)
- Analytical review (average score of 3.21)

When comparing the 21 European countries, we notice:

- a high current use of **analytical review** in Cyprus, Czech Republic, Germany, Romania and Turkey;
- a high current use of **balanced scorecard** in Belgium, Finland, France, Romania and Spain;
- a high current use of **benchmarking** in Bulgaria, Estonia, Finland Turkey, and Sweden;
- a high current use of **Computer Assisted Audit Techniques** in Austria, Germany, Portugal, Switzerland and Turkey;
- a high current use of **continuous / real-time auditing** in Austria, Bulgaria, Germany, Greece and Turkey;
- a high current use of **Control Self Assessment** in Czech Republic, Estonia, Turkey, Poland and Netherlands;
- a high current use of **data mining** in Czech Republic, France, Greece, Poland and Turkey;
- a high current use of **electronic work papers** in Czech Republic, France, Greece, Italy and Norway;
- a high current use of **flowchart software** in Estonia, Italy, Portugal, Switzerland and Turkey;
- a high current use of **other electronic communication** (e.g. Internet, email) in Czech Republic, Estonia, Finland, Germany and Sweden;
- a high current use of **process mapping application** in Bulgaria, France, Greece, Italy, Spain;
- a high current use of **process modeling software** in Greece, Italy, Romania, Spain and Switzerland;
- a high current use of **risk based audit planning** in Estonia, Germany, Sweden, Switzerland and UK & Ireland;
- a high current use of **statistical sampling** in Czech Republic, Poland, Portugal, Spain and Turkey;
- a high current use of **The IIA's quality assessment review tools** in Belgium, Czech Republic, Estonia, Finland and Switzerland;
- a high current use of **total quality management techniques** in Bulgaria, Czech Republic, Finland, Netherlands and Turkey.

Table 51 shows that the following audit tools are **planned** to be most extensively used in **the next three years**:

- Other electronic communication (e.g., Internet, email) (average score of 4.16)
- Risk based audit planning (average score of 4.00)
- Electronic work papers (average score of 3.69);
- Analytical review (average score of 3.35);
- Computer Assisted Audit Techniques (CAAT) (average score of 3.14).

It is worth mentioning that for all audit tools, there is an expected increase in the use. The tools with the highest increase are:

- The IIA's quality assessment review tools;
- Computer Assisted Audit Techniques;
- Control Self Assessment;
- Risk based audit planning;
- Total quality management techniques.

Table 51: Planned Use of Internal Audit Tools (means)

Country	Analytical review	Balanced scorecard or similar framework	Benchmarking	Computer Assisted Audit Techniques	Continuous / real-time auditing	Control Self Assessment	Data mining	Electronic work papers
Austria	3.48	2.17	2.98	3.69	2.97	2.28	2.43	3.21
Belgium	3.44	2.43	2.72	3.09	2.41	2.81	3.00	3.75
Bulgaria	3.78	2.86	3.38	3.58	3.44	3.35	3.31	3.88
Cyprus	4.00	2.22	3.28	3.11	2.83	2.78	2.71	3.28
Czech Republic	3.95	2.54	2.96	3.08	2.81	3.01	2.82	4.08
Estonia	3.00	2.13	2.29	3.00	2.75	2.86	2.67	4.13
Finland	3.71	2.83	3.19	3.50	2.81	3.16	2.81	3.66
France	3.16	2.76	2.94	3.09	2.12	3.01	3.62	3.95
Germany	3.75	2.03	2.77	3.51	2.70	2.55	2.58	3.48
Greece	3.68	2.29	2.93	3.54	3.41	2.61	2.95	3.98
Italy	3.09	1.83	2.39	2.57	2.20	2.72	2.09	3.80
Netherlands	3.46	2.25	2.68	3.21	2.43	2.96	2.62	3.69
Norway	3.26	2.41	2.77	2.68	2.00	2.45	1.86	3.77
Poland	3.37	2.38	2.58	3.27	2.71	3.25	3.46	3.89
Portugal	3.16	2.12	2.79	3.27	2.85	2.80	2.38	3.50
Romania	3.79	3.06	3.32	3.90	3.42	3.30	3.32	3.95
Spain	2.74	2.47	2.12	2.64	2.34	2.22	2.06	2.99
Sweden	3.58	1.93	2.93	3.19	2.21	2.86	1.85	3.49
Switzerland	3.64	2.14	2.83	3.33	2.67	2.59	2.81	3.63
Turkey	4.21	2.46	3.40	4.33	3.64	3.59	3.80	4.05
UK & Ireland	2.99	2.11	2.69	3.17	2.44	2.67	2.40	3.87
Overall average	**3.35**	**2.31**	**2.74**	**3.14**	**2.56**	**2.77**	**2.67**	**3.69**

1 = Not Used, 2 = Moderately Used, 3 = Average Use,
4 = Very Much Used, 5 = Extensively Used

Country	Flowchart software	Other electronic communication (e.g. Internet, email)	Process mapping application	Process modeling software	Risk based audit planning	Statistical sampling	The IIA's Quality Assessment Review tools	Total quality management techniques
Austria	2.27	4.17	2.85	2.44	4.11	3.11	2.34	2.02
Belgium	2.54	4.22	2.75	1.88	4.15	2.72	2.63	2.25
Bulgaria	3.43	4.06	3.54	2.76	4.00	3.25	3.30	3.30
Cyprus	2.89	4.22	3.22	2.06	4.00	3.35	3.06	2.67
Czech Republic	3.07	4.37	3.07	2.27	4.32	3.29	3.14	2.81
Estonia	2.86	4.43	2.88	1.50	4.14	2.63	2.63	2.50
Finland	2.52	4.38	2.50	2.25	4.16	2.77	3.19	2.56
France	2.32	4.29	3.19	2.17	4.01	2.81	2.16	2.01
Germany	2.67	4.29	3.04	2.42	4.27	3.16	2.59	2.28
Greece	2.65	4.57	3.07	2.31	4.00	3.08	2.79	2.60
Italy	2.72	3.95	2.87	2.01	3.73	2.87	2.32	1.79
Netherlands	2.32	4.34	2.55	2.03	4.06	2.70	2.61	2.25
Norway	1.95	4.18	2.14	1.62	4.14	2.32	2.39	1.83
Poland	3.16	4.54	3.13	2.92	4.35	3.49	2.50	2.46
Portugal	2.83	4.24	2.87	2.22	3.82	3.08	2.55	2.44
Romania	3.55	4.11	3.75	3.50	4.00	3.33	3.33	3.10
Spain	2.08	3.27	2.38	1.84	3.22	2.56	1.97	1.82
Sweden	2.25	4.62	2.00	1.59	4.29	2.38	2.88	1.78
Switzerland	2.55	4.17	2.93	2.36	4.33	2.97	2.79	2.07
Turkey	3.10	4.35	3.11	2.57	4.13	3.54	2.89	3.03
UK & Ireland	2.30	4.35	2.41	1.67	4.32	2.69	2.14	2.08
Overall average	**2.56**	**4.16**	**2.81**	**2.12**	**4.00**	**2.90**	**2.50**	**2.21**

When comparing the planned use of audit tools between all 21 European countries, we notice:

- a high increase in the planned use of **analytical review** in Cyprus, Finland and Switzerland;
- a high increase in the planned use of **balanced scorecard** in Bulgaria, Poland and Romania;
- a high increase in the planned use of **benchmarking** in Cyprus, Poland and Romania;

- a high increase in the planned use of **Computer Assisted Audit Techniques** in Bulgaria, Cyprus and Romania;
- a high increase in the planned use of **continuous / real-time auditing** in Bulgaria, Romania and Turkey;
- a high increase in the planned use of **Control Self Assessment** in Bulgaria, Cyprus and Turkey;
- a high increase in the planned use of **data mining** in Bulgaria, Finland and Romania;
- a high increase in the planned use of **electronic work papers** in Bulgaria, Poland and Romania;
- a high increase in the planned use of **flowchart software** in Bulgaria, Poland and Romania;
- a high increase in the planned use of **other electronic communication** (e.g. Internet, email) in Bulgaria, Poland and Romania;
- a high increase in the planned use of **process mapping application** in Bulgaria, Poland and Romania;
- a high increase in the planned use of **process modeling software** in Bulgaria, Poland and Romania;
- a high increase in the planned use of **risk based audit planning** Bulgaria, Cyprus and Turkey;
- a high increase in the planned use of **statistical sampling** in Bulgaria, Cyprus and Romania;
- a high increase in the planned use of **The IIA's quality assessment review tools** in Bulgaria, Cyprus and Romania;
- a high increase in the planned use of **total quality management techniques** in Bulgaria, Cyprus and Romania.

7.2.   Behavioural Skills

From the 12 behavioural skills that were listed in Table 52, CAEs were asked to indicate the five most important for the various professional staff levels in the IAF. Overall, the results show that:

The five most important behavioural skills for **audit staff** are:

- Confidentiality (74%), except in Bulgaria, Sweden and UK & Ireland.
- Objectivity (74%), except in Bulgaria, Greece and Netherlands;
- Team player (66%), except in Belgium, Finland and Turkey;
- Interpersonal skill (59%), except in Belgium, Greece and Turkey;
- Working independently (54%), except in Bulgaria, Greece and Italy.

The five most important behavioural skills for **seniors / supervisors** are:

- Confidentiality (57%), except in Bulgaria, Estonia and Sweden;
- Objectivity (56%), except in Bulgaria, Estonia and Finland;
- Interpersonal skill (43%), except in Germany, Greece and Sweden;
- Team player (39%), except in Estonia, Finland and Sweden;
- Work well with all level of management (32%), except in Bulgaria, Estonia, and Netherlands.

The five most important behavioural skills for **managers** are:

- Confidentiality (51%), except in Finland, Portugal and Turkey;
- Objectivity (45%), except in Estonia, Finland and UK & Ireland;
- Staff management (45%), except in Estonia, Finland and Norway;
- Leadership (43%), except in Germany, Netherlands and Norway;
- Team building (41%), except in Estonia, Sweden and Turkey.

The five most important behavioural skills for **CAEs** are:

- Leadership (71%), except in Czech Republic, Estonia and Norway;
- Confidentiality (70%), except in Finland, Portugal and Sweden;
- Objectivity (62%), except in Sweden, Switzerland and UK & Ireland;
- Governance and ethics sensitivity (57%), except in Cyprus, Finland and Poland;
- Work well with all level of management (52%), except in France, Romania, and Spain.

Table 52: Behavioural Skills (%)

Country	Total Number of Respondents	Confidentiality				Facilitating				Governance and ethics sensitivity				Interpersonal skills			
		Audit staff	Senior	Mgr	CAE	Audit staff	Senior	Mgr	CAE	Audit staff	Senior	Mgr	CAE	Audit staff	Senior	Mgr	CAE
Austria	46	82.6	78.3	60.9	80.4	13.0	39.1	30.4	37.0	6.5	19.6	28.3	52.2	58.7	34.8	30.4	23.9
Belgium	19	68.4	42.1	47.4	63.2	10.5	26.3	47.4	36.8	31.6	21.1	52.6	68.4	42.1	42.1	26.3	36.8
Bulgaria	21	52.4	33.3	52.4	81.0	28.6	33.3	42.9	52.4	52.4	28.6	52.4	71.4	52.4	38.1	52.4	66.7
Cyprus	6	83.3	83.3	66.7	83.3	33.3	33.3	50.0	33.3	0.0	0.0	16.7	33.3	66.7	66.7	50.0	66.7
Czech Republic	59	78.0	66.1	44.1	71.2	27.1	50.8	44.1	47.5	22.0	50.8	32.2	55.9	64.4	42.4	39.0	45.8
Estonia	6	83.3	33.3	33.3	66.7	50.0	0.0	16.7	33.3	16.7	16.7	0.0	33.3	83.3	33.3	33.3	33.3
Finland	13	53.8	38.5	15.4	53.8	7.7	15.4	0.0	0.0	30.8	0.0	7.7	15.4	61.5	38.5	30.8	61.5
France	74	79.7	58.1	43.2	67.6	9.5	28.4	41.9	43.2	21.6	23.0	48.6	56.8	78.4	45.9	16.2	20.3
Germany	36	66.7	47.2	38.9	63.9	8.3	36.1	25.0	47.2	22.2	27.8	30.6	47.2	55.6	27.8	25.0	38.9
Greece	12	75.0	66.7	66.7	83.3	16.7	41.7	25.0	16.7	16.7	16.7	25.0	50.0	25.0	25.0	25.0	41.7
Italy	107	74.8	58.9	62.6	83.2	20.6	26.2	34.6	37.4	32.7	28.0	43.0	66.4	50.5	43.0	41.1	52.3
Netherlands	26	73.1	65.4	73.1	80.8	11.5	11.5	23.1	23.1	30.8	30.8	19.2	46.2	57.7	57.7	50.0	69.2
Norway	10	80.0	50.0	50.0	60.0	40.0	40.0	20.0	20.0	10.0	10.0	30.0	50.0	60.0	60.0	70.0	50.0
Poland	8	62.5	62.5	62.5	87.5	25.0	37.5	37.5	87.5	0.0	12.5	25.0	25.0	50.0	50.0	75.0	100.0
Portugal	15	80.0	66.7	26.7	53.3	20.0	20.0	40.0	26.7	13.3	33.3	60.0	73.3	60.0	33.3	40.0	26.7
Romania	4	100.0	75.0	100.0	75.0	25.0	0.0	25.0	50.0	25.0	25.0	25.0	1000	100.0	75.0	50.0	25.0
Spain	83	84.3	63.9	59.0	73.5	16.9	21.7	30.1	32.5	31.3	28.9	31.3	62.7	55.4	38.6	36.1	42.2
Sweden	18	55.6	27.8	33.3	50.0	11.1	0.0	5.6	16.7	33.3	27.8	44.4	50.0	55.6	27.8	27.8	22.2
Switzerland	15	86.7	66.7	53.3	60.0	0.0	33.3	40.0	46.7	33.3	60.0	60.0	73.3	53.3	26.7	26.7	53.3
Turkey	27	74.1	44.4	29.6	55.6	18.5	44.4	44.4	22.2	40.7	48.1	51.9	59.3	44.4	37.0	18.5	25.9
UK & Ireland	67	59.7	46.3	43.3	55.2	13.4	25.4	32.8	26.9	9.0	9.0	17.9	46.3	73.1	64.2	67.2	50.7
Overall Average	**672**	**74.1**	**57.1**	**50.6**	**70.2**	**16.8**	**29.2**	**33.6**	**35.7**	**24.6**	**27.1**	**35.7**	**56.5**	**59.4**	**42.9**	**37.6**	**42.7**

Note that only CAEs responded to this question.

Country	Leadership				Objectivity				Relationship building				Staff management			
	Audit staff	Senior	Mgr	CAE	Audit staff	Senior	Mgr	CAE	Audit staff	Senior	Mgr	CAE	Audit staff	Senior	Mgr	CAE
Austria	2.2	26.1	41.3	69.6	80.4	76.1	45.7	65.2	28.3	13.0	17.4	26.1	2.2	34.8	41.3	50.0
Belgium	0.0	21.1	36.8	78.9	78.9	47.4	36.8	47.4	26.3	26.3	36.8	31.6	0.0	26.3	52.6	47.4
Bulgaria	4.8	4.8	52.4	71.4	52.4	33.3	42.9	71.4	38.1	38.1	38.1	61.9	0.0	9.5	52.4	71.4
Cyprus	16.7	33.3	50.0	83.3	66.7	50.0	50.0	66.7	33.3	50.0	33.3	16.7	0.0	16.7	50.0	66.7
Czech Republic	0.0	1.7	50.8	49.2	81.4	71.2	54.2	69.5	28.8	23.7	25.4	27.1	0.0	11.9	59.3	54.2
Estonia	16.7	0.0	50.0	33.3	83.3	33.3	33.3	83.3	50.0	0.0	0.0	66.7	0.0	16.7	0.0	33.3
Finland	0.0	15.4	38.5	53.8	61.5	15.4	23.1	53.8	30.8	15.4	23.1	23.1	0.0	0.0	15.4	23.1
France	1.4	32.4	45.9	59.5	74.3	58.1	44.6	70.3	27.0	13.5	32.4	36.5	0.0	16.2	37.8	41.9
Germany	0.0	11.1	25.0	61.1	75.0	47.2	41.7	66.7	11.1	13.9	27.8	52.8	0.0	30.6	25.0	55.6
Greece	0.0	16.7	58.3	83.3	50.0	50.0	58.3	75.0	25.0	50.0	41.7	25.0	0.0	33.3	16.7	33.3
Italy	3.7	15.9	49.5	77.6	65.4	54.2	51.4	65.4	31.8	25.2	37.4	52.3	1.9	26.2	53.3	54.2
Netherlands	0.0	7.7	23.1	76.9	53.8	57.7	46.2	53.8	30.8	30.8	26.9	38.5	0.0	19.2	26.9	7.7
Norway	0.0	0.0	0.0	40.0	80.0	70.0	60.0	70.0	30.0	20.0	20.0	30.0	0.0	20.0	10.0	20.0
Poland	0.0	25.0	75.0	87.5	75.0	37.5	25.0	75.0	50.0	50.0	50.0	100.0	12.5	12.5	62.5	100.0
Portugal	0.0	20.0	53.3	73.3	80.0	66.7	40.0	66.7	33.3	26.7	33.3	20.0	0.0	20.0	40.0	40.0
Romania	0.0	0.0	100.0	100.0	75.0	50.0	50.0	50.0	25.0	25.0	25.0	50.0	0.0	0.0	50.0	50.0
Spain	1.2	14.5	34.9	81.9	83.1	63.9	42.2	55.4	21.7	22.9	27.7	39.8	2.4	32.5	39.8	56.6
Sweden	0.0	38.9	38.9	66.7	83.3	33.3	38.9	38.9	33.3	38.9	22.2	50.0	0.0	16.7	27.8	44.4
Switzerland	0.0	13.3	66.7	80.0	86.7	86.7	53.3	46.7	20.0	26.7	40.0	53.3	0.0	46.7	60.0	53.3
Turkey	7.4	18.5	44.4	70.4	81.5	40.7	40.7	66.7	55.6	18.5	22.2	33.3	7.4	37.0	48.1	33.3
UK & Ireland	1.5	10.4	38.8	85.1	68.7	46.3	38.8	46.3	52.2	46.3	53.7	68.7	1.5	32.8	65.7	37.3
Overall Average	1.9	16.2	43.0	71.1	73.5	55.8	44.9	61.6	31.4	25.4	32.1	43.3	1.3	24.9	44.8	47.3

Note that only CAEs responded to this question.

111

Country	Team building				Team player				Working independently				Work well with all levels of management			
	Audit staff	Senior	Mgr	CAE	Audit staff	Senior	Mgr	CAE	Audit staff	Senior	Mgr	CAE	Audit staff	Senior	Mgr	CAE
Austria	8.7	15.2	41.3	26.1	65.2	30.4	10.9	8.7	67.4	39.1	13.0	10.9	37.0	28.3	28.3	60.9
Belgium	0.0	63.2	36.8	15.8	52.6	36.8	15.8	15.8	63.2	31.6	15.8	21.1	42.1	36.8	26.3	73.7
Bulgaria	57.1	42.9	33.3	57.1	66.7	42.9	19.0	52.4	28.6	23.8	38.1	71.4	19.0	19.0	57.1	66.7
Cyprus	16.7	33.3	33.3	16.7	66.7	66.7	50.0	33.3	50.0	16.7	0.0	33.3	33.3	50.0	66.7	83.3
Czech Republic	6.8	6.8	47.5	35.6	78.0	20.3	32.2	25.4	81.4	35.6	20.3	18.6	25.4	37.3	40.7	61.0
Estonia	16.7	0.0	16.7	66.7	66.7	16.7	16.7	33.3	50.0	16.7	16.7	33.3	0.0	0.0	33.3	50.0
Finland	0.0	23.1	46.2	0.0	23.1	23.1	15.4	7.7	30.8	23.1	15.4	30.8	7.7	23.1	15.4	61.5
France	5.4	37.8	33.8	33.8	51.4	28.4	13.5	14.9	48.6	33.8	21.6	36.5	47.3	24.3	23.0	29.7
Germany	0.0	33.3	33.3	30.6	55.6	41.7	13.9	8.3	75.0	44.4	19.4	30.6	41.7	27.8	33.3	58.3
Greece	8.3	16.7	41.7	25.0	66.7	33.3	16.7	16.7	33.3	16.7	8.3	8.3	66.7	50.0	33.3	50.0
Italy	15.0	30.8	48.6	56.1	75.7	44.9	32.7	30.8	39.3	31.8	25.2	27.1	39.3	37.4	40.2	51.4
Netherlands	3.8	11.5	50.0	26.9	65.4	42.3	11.5	7.7	65.4	34.6	15.4	15.4	30.8	19.2	26.9	34.6
Norway	0.0	10.0	40.0	20.0	50.0	40.0	20.0	30.0	40.0	30.0	40.0	10.0	60.0	60.0	90.0	100
Poland	25.0	25.0	37.5	87.5	75.0	50.0	37.5	62.5	75.0	12.5	12.5	62.5	50.0	25.0	50.0	100
Portugal	6.7	26.7	40.0	6.7	73.3	40.0	13.3	6.7	40.0	33.3	20.0	20.0	40.0	20.0	26.7	53.3
Romania	0.0	0.0	100.0	75.0	75.0	50.0	0.0	0.0	50.0	50.0	50.0	50.0	25.0	25.0	50.0	25.0
Spain	2.4	24.1	41.0	43.4	72.3	51.8	32.5	21.7	39.8	14.5	9.6	18.1	34.9	21.7	32.5	33.7
Sweden	5.6	11.1	22.2	38.9	55.6	16.7	0.0	0.0	61.1	0.0	0.0	5.6	33.3	38.9	33.3	77.8
Switzerland	0.0	20.0	53.3	26.7	93.3	53.3	26.7	26.7	86.7	40.0	20.0	33.3	60.0	60.0	53.3	53.3
Turkey	11.1	44.4	14.8	40.7	33.3	33.3	7.4	7.4	44.4	3.7	7.4	29.6	29.6	29.6	22.2	48.1
UK & Ireland	1.5	26.9	43.3	31.3	76.1	46.3	22.4	10.4	59.7	26.9	10.4	9.0	52.2	49.3	55.2	61.2
Overall Average	8.0	26.3	40.6	37.4	66.1	38.5	21.9	19.2	53.6	28.1	17.4	24.0	38.5	32.4	36.9	52.4

Note that only CAEs responded to this question.

7.3.   Technical Skills

From the 13 technical skills that are listed in Table 53, CAEs were asked to indicate the five most important technical skills for the various professional staff levels in the IAF. Overall, the results show that:

The five most important technical skills for **audit staff** are:

- Data collection and analysis (76%), except in Bulgaria and Norway;
- Interviewing (61%), except in Finland, Spain and Turkey;
- Use of information technology (55%), except in Cyprus, Netherlands and Sweden;
- Identifying types of controls (45%), except in Austria, Czech Republic and Finland;
- Understanding business (41%), except in Cyprus, Czech Republic and Romania.

The five most important technical skills for **seniors / supervisors** are:

- Interviewing (46%), except in Bulgaria, Estonia and Finland;
- Identifying type of controls (44%), except in Bulgaria, Finland and Poland;
- Risk analysis (43%), except in Germany, Finland and Poland;
- Understanding business (42%), except in Bulgaria, Czech Republic and France;
- Financial analysis (33%), except in Cyprus, Norway and Sweden.

The five most important technical skills for **managers** are:

- Understanding business (57%), except in Austria, Estonia and Turkey;
- Risk analysis (56%), except in Estonia, Finland and Germany;
- Negotiating (50%), except in Cyprus, Finland and Norway;
- Interviewing (39%), except in Estonia, Finland and Germany;
- Forensic skills / fraud awareness (34%), except in Estonia, Finland, and Turkey.

The five most important technical skills for **CAEs** are:

- Understanding business (76%), except in Czech Republic, Romania and Turkey;
- Risk analysis (75%), except in Belgium, Czech Republic and Poland;
- Negotiating (73%), except in Cyprus, Norway and Romania;
- Interviewing (44%), except in Estonia, Greece and Portugal;
- Forensic skills / fraud awareness (37%) except in Finland, Turkey and UK & Ireland.

Table 53: Technical Skills (%)

Country	Total Number of respondents	Data collection and analysis				Financial analysis				Forensic skills / Fraud awareness				Identifying types of controls			
		Audit staff	Senior	Mgr	CAE	Audit staff	Senior	Mgr	CAE	Audit staff	Senior	Mgr	CAE	Audit staff	Senior	Mgr	CAE
Austria	46	80.4	37.0	17.4	8.7	17.8	21.7	30.4	37.0	34.8	43.5	32.6	37.0	23.9	43.5	30.4	39.1
Belgium	19	78.9	36.8	0.0	5.3	15.8	47.4	47.4	47.4	21.1	26.3	26.3	36.8	52.6	57.9	15.8	10.5
Bulgaria	21	66.7	33.3	33.3	57.1	33.3	23.8	28.6	52.4	38.1	28.6	38.1	71.4	42.9	23.8	42.9	66.7
Cyprus	6	66.7	33.3	0.0	33.3	50.0	16.7	16.7	33.3	33.3	33.3	33.3	33.3	83.3	66.7	50.0	50.0
Czech Republic	59	88.1	30.5	10.2	18.6	33.9	37.3	45.8	28.8	20.3	33.9	35.6	52.5	23.7	35.6	20.3	23.7
Estonia	6	83.3	33.3	0.0	16.7	33.3	33.3	16.7	33.3	16.7	16.7	16.7	50.0	50.0	50.0	33.3	33.3
Finland	13	53.8	23.1	7.7	7.7	30.8	30.8	15.4	30.8	7.7	7.7	15.4	15.4	23.1	23.1	7.7	46.2
France	74	74.2	29.7	2.7	6.8	31.1	36.5	25.7	39.2	12.2	17.6	31.1	39.2	40.5	43.2	20.3	29.7
Germany	36	72.2	19.4	11.1	11.1	25.0	27.8	13.9	19.4	19.4	25.0	33.3	38.9	38.9	27.8	25.0	27.8
Greece	12	66.7	41.7	16.7	0.0	41.7	58.3	33.3	33.3	0.0	0.0	41.7	41.7	41.7	66.7	50.0	16.7
Italy	107	72.9	35.5	28.0	23.4	22.4	26.2	40.2	38.3	11.2	29.9	44.9	49.5	41.1	43.9	46.7	45.8
Netherlands	26	73.1	26.9	11.5	19.2	42.3	50.0	30.8	42.3	11.5	15.4	30.8	30.8	42.3	38.5	30.8	34.6
Norway	10	50.0	20.0	30.0	10.0	10.0	20.0	20.0	20.0	30.0	50.0	60.0	60.0	60.0	40.0	40.0	30.0
Poland	8	87.5	25.0	12.5	37.5	37.5	50.0	50.0	62.5	62.5	37.5	62.5	50.0	37.5	25.0	50.0	37.5
Portugal	15	80.0	26.7	26.7	26.7	26.7	40.0	46.7	40.0	20.0	40.0	46.7	40.0	66.7	46.7	33.3	26.7
Romania	4	75.0	50.0	0.0	0.0	25.0	75.0	25.0	50.0	25.0	50.0	50.0	50.0	75.0	50.0	25.0	0.0
Spain	83	79.5	22.9	6.0	7.2	50.6	38.6	25.3	21.7	14.5	26.5	20.5	15.7	56.6	47.0	39.8	34.9
Sweden	18	77.8	16.7	11.1	22.2	16.7	16.7	33.3	33.3	11.1	16.7	27.8	33.3	61.1	33.3	22.2	38.9
Switzerland	15	86.7	40.0	13.3	20.0	40.0	46.7	20.0	33.3	13.3	26.7	33.3	33.3	33.3	53.3	26.7	20.0
Turkey	27	66.7	25.9	3.7	18.5	40.7	33.3	37.0	44.4	25.9	33.3	18.5	29.6	44.4	33.3	37.0	59.3
UK & Ireland	67	74.6	38.8	13.4	7.5	26.9	29.9	28.4	32.8	10.4	19.4	35.8	22.4	73.1	61.2	41.8	17.9
Overall Average	672	75.6	30.7	13.4	15.2	31.0	33.3	31.5	34.5	17.4	26.8	33.6	37.4	45.4	43.5	33.5	33.9

Note that only CAEs responded to this question.

Country	Interviewing				ISO / quality knowledge				Negotiating				Research skills			
	Audit staff	Senior	Mgr	CAE	Audit staff	Senior	Mgr	CAE	Audit staff	Senior	Mgr	CAE	Audit staff	Senior	Mgr	CAE
Austria	58.7	56.5	34.8	39.1	4.3	4.3	17.4	17.4	19.6	47.8	39.1	69.6	63.0	32.6	13.0	23.9
Belgium	68.4	47.4	36.8	36.8	0.0	10.5	10.5	15.8	0.0	26.3	63.2	84.2	31.6	15.8	10.5	5.3
Bulgaria	52.4	19.0	28.6	66.7	28.6	23.8	38.1	61.9	14.3	14.3	52.4	76.2	33.3	23.8	28.6	47.6
Cyprus	50.0	66.7	66.7	66.7	0.0	0.0	0.0	0.0	16.7	0.0	0.0	50.0	0.0	16.7	16.7	0.0
Czech Republic	72.9	35.6	50.8	59.3	18.6	37.3	30.5	30.5	22.0	22.0	62.7	69.5	62.7	50.8	25.4	30.5
Estonia	83.3	0.0	0.0	16.7	16.7	0.0	0.0	33.3	33.3	0.0	50.0	83.3	33.3	16.7	16.7	33.3
Finland	38.5	15.4	7.7	38.5	0.0	7.7	0.0	7.7	0.0	15.4	23.1	61.5	30.8	15.4	15.4	0.0
France	63.5	48.6	35.1	45.9	6.8	5.4	12.2	10.8	2.7	27.0	51.4	73.0	24.3	17.6	5.4	8.1
Germany	52.8	52.8	19.4	27.8	2.8	8.3	22.2	13.9	8.3	41.7	36.1	66.7	52.8	47.2	19.4	19.4
Greece	50.0	41.7	25.0	16.7	8.3	8.3	8.3	8.3	0.0	0.0	50.0	75.0	50.0	41.7	16.7	8.3
Italy	62.6	49.5	40.2	33.6	12.1	13.1	16.8	22.4	13.1	21.5	46.7	76.6	54.2	45.8	31.8	34.6
Netherlands	73.1	46.2	38.5	34.6	11.5	7.7	7.7	3.8	7.7	19.2	38.5	65.4	23.1	23.1	23.1	19.2
Norway	70.0	80.0	50.0	50.0	0.0	0.0	10.0	20.0	10.0	20.0	20.0	30.0	20.0	20.0	10.0	30.0
Poland	62.5	25.0	37.5	75.0	37.5	37.5	25.0	25.0	12.5	50.0	62.5	87.5	50.0	37.5	25.0	50.0
Portugal	53.3	53.3	40.0	6.7	0.0	13.3	33.3	33.3	6.7	13.3	46.7	60.0	33.3	33.3	26.7	20.0
Romania	100.0	75.0	25.0	50.0	0.0	0.0	75.0	50.0	0.0	25.0	75.0	50.0	75.0	25.0	25.0	0.0
Spain	39.8	41.0	50.6	50.6	8.4	8.4	20.5	26.5	8.4	21.7	50.6	79.5	30.1	37.3	18.1	13.3
Sweden	77.8	27.8	27.8	66.7	0.0	0.0	0.0	5.6	5.6	22.2	27.8	61.1	5.6	0.0	11.1	0.0
Switzerland	86.7	60.0	53.3	53.3	0.0	6.7	13.3	26.7	6.7	33.3	73.3	73.3	46.7	13.3	26.7	20.0
Turkey	29.6	22.2	37.0	55.6	11.1	25.9	11.1	14.8	18.5	25.9	44.4	55.6	40.7	25.9	3.7	18.5
UK & Ireland	80.6	62.7	47.8	43.3	3.0	3.0	11.9	14.9	9.0	31.3	71.6	83.6	28.4	14.9	13.4	23.9
Overall Average	61.2	45.8	39.4	43.9	8.6	11.6	17.1	20.2	10.7	25.6	50.0	72.5	40.0	31.0	18.6	21.3

Note that only CAEs responded to this question.

115

Country	Risk analysis				Statistical sampling				Total Quality Management			
	Audit staff	Senior	Mgr	CAE	Audit staff	Senior	Mgr	CAE	Audit staff	Senior	Mgr	CAE
Austria	17.4	26.1	45.7	67.4	32.6	17.4	10.9	6.5	2.2	6.5	10.9	23.9
Belgium	31.6	52.6	68.4	63.2	36.8	21.1	15.8	0.0	0.0	0.0	31.6	52.6
Bulgaria	42.9	28.6	42.9	76.2	23.8	28.6	23.8	47.6	23.8	19.0	47.6	61.9
Cyprus	33.3	83.3	83.3	100.0	33.3	16.7	16.7	16.7	0.0	16.7	16.7	33.3
Czech Republic	22.0	27.1	40.7	49.2	40.7	18.6	3.4	1.7	1.7	16.9	47.5	62.7
Estonia	50.0	33.3	33.3	83.3	16.7	0.0	16.7	16.7	16.7	16.7	16.7	33.3
Finland	30.8	23.1	38.5	69.2	7.7	0.0	0.0	0.0	0.0	7.7	15.4	7.7
France	47.3	56.8	52.7	83.8	28.4	16.2	0.0	0.0	4.1	16.2	20.3	25.7
Germany	22.2	22.2	30.6	69.4	22.2	27.8	5.6	0.0	0.0	0.0	19.4	22.2
Greece	0.0	33.3	75.0	83.3	41.7	8.3	0.0	0.0	0.0	8.3	25.0	50.0
Italy	28.0	45.8	64.5	76.6	36.4	30.8	25.2	14.0	7.5	10.3	16.8	23.4
Netherlands	34.6	61.5	69.2	73.1	15.4	19.2	11.5	0.0	3.8	11.5	11.5	46.2
Norway	80.0	50.0	70.0	90.0	0.0	0.0	0.0	0.0	0.0	0.0	20.0	30.0
Poland	50.0	12.5	62.5	62.5	50.0	25.0	25.6	50.0	25.0	25.0	50.0	50.0
Portugal	46.7	66.7	73.3	73.3	40.0	20.0	6.7	20.0	0.0	13.3	33.3	33.3
Romania	0.0	75.0	50.0	100.0	25.0	50.0	0.0	0.0	0.0	0.0	50.0	75.0
Spain	27.7	39.8	54.2	85.5	39.8	16.9	7.2	4.8	3.6	6.0	14.5	36.1
Sweden	55.6	44.4	38.9	66.7	5.6	5.6	5.6	0.0	0.0	5.6	5.6	16.7
Switzerland	26.7	60.0	60.0	86.7	20.0	26.7	20.0	13.3	6.7	20.0	13.3	20.0
Turkey	48.1	37.0	63.0	74.1	29.6	11.1	7.4	11.1	7.4	18.5	37.0	37.0
UK & Ireland	41.8	50.7	70.1	79.1	16.4	7.5	3.0	1.5	4.5	6.0	10.4	22.4
Overall Average	33.3	42.6	55.8	75.0	29.6	18.6	9.8	7.1	4.6	10.3	21.4	33.0

Note that only CAEs responded to this question.

7.4.   Competencies

From the 18 competences that are listed in Table 54, CAEs were asked to indicate the five most important competencies for the various professional staff levels in the IAF. Overall, the results show that:

The five most important competencies for **audit staff** are:

- Analytical (ability to work through an issue) (63%), except in Cyprus, Poland and Switzerland.
- Writing skills (47%), except in Cyprus, Finland and Romania;
- Critical thinking (46%), except in Bulgaria, Poland and Turkey;
- Communication (45%), except in Belgium, Portugal and Spain;
- Problem identification and solution (42%), except in Bulgaria, Greece and Spain.

The five most important competences for **seniors / supervisors** are:

- Analytical (45%), except in Bulgaria, Poland and Turkey;
- Communication (38%), except in Finland, Portugal and Romania;
- Critical thinking (34%), except in Bulgaria, Finland and UK & Ireland;
- Problem identification and solution (33%), except in Austria, Estonia and Greece;
- Keeping up to date with professional changes in opinions, standards and regulations (27%) except in Belgium, Greece and Sweden.

The five most important competences for **managers** are:

- Communication (44%), except in Austria, Finland and Turkey;
- Conflict resolution (34%), except in Netherlands, Norway and Sweden;
- Organization skills (30%), except in Estonia, Finland and Norway;
- Keeping up to date with professional changes in opinions, standards and regulations (30%) except in Cyprus, Estonia and Sweden;
- Ability to promote the IAF within the organization (29%), except in Czech Republic, Finland and Romania.

The five most important competences for **CAEs** are:

- Ability to promote the IAF within the organization (80%), except in Estonia, Finland and Norway;
- Communication (58%), except in Austria, Turkey and Germany;
- Conflict resolution (46%), except in Cyprus, Finland and Norway;
- Organization skills (40%), except in Finland, Sweden and UK & Ireland;
- Keeping up to date with professional changes in opinions, standards and regulations (36%) except in Cyprus, Germany and Netherlands.

Table 54: Competencies (%)

Country	Total Number of Respondents	Ability to promote the IAF within the organization				Analytical				Change Management				Communication			
		Audit staff	Senior	Mgr	CAE	Audit staff	Senior	Mgr	CAE	Audit staff	Senior	Mgr	CAE	Audit staff	Senior	Mgr	CAE
Austria	46	13.0	8.7	21.7	73.9	67.4	60.9	23.9	21.7	4.3	4.3	17.4	34.8	52.2	43.5	32.6	32.6
Belgium	19	5.3	5.3	26.3	84.2	63.2	42.1	15.8	0.0	5.3	5.3	21.1	36.8	15.8	31.6	36.8	68.4
Bulgaria	21	19.0	14.3	52.4	71.4	57.1	33.3	38.1	66.7	14.3	19.0	42.9	61.9	61.9	38.1	52.4	71.4
Cyprus	6	16.7	16.7	50.0	83.3	83.3	83.3	33.3	16.7	0.0	0.0	0.0	0.0	50.0	66.7	66.7	50.0
Czech Republic	59	3.4	8.5	13.6	84.7	79.7	42.4	33.9	22.0	8.5	13.6	20.3	10.2	72.9	45.8	49.2	50.8
Estonia	6	0.0	16.7	16.7	66.7	83.3	33.3	0.0	33.3	16.7	0.0	16.7	16.7	83.3	33.3	50.0	66.7
Finland	13	7.7	7.7	7.7	38.5	61.5	38.5	15.4	30.8	0.0	7.7	15.4	0.0	46.2	23.1	30.8	76.9
France	74	9.5	16.2	43.2	75.7	45.9	37.8	24.3	25.7	4.1	6.8	21.6	17.6	33.8	36.5	37.8	60.8
Germany	36	11.1	8.3	25.0	80.6	63.9	41.7	13.9	19.4	0.0	5.6	11.1	25.0	50.0	36.1	41.7	47.2
Greece	12	0.0	0.0	16.7	66.7	58.3	66.7	25.0	8.3	0.0	8.3	25.0	16.7	66.7	50.0	33.3	50.0
Italy	107	10.3	8.4	26.2	85.0	60.7	47.7	31.8	22.4	8.4	11.2	37.4	61.7	28.0	31.8	49.5	64.5
Netherlands	26	0.0	0.0	26.9	84.6	69.2	53.8	26.9	19.2	3.8	7.7	11.5	30.8	53.8	42.3	38.5	61.5
Norway	13	10.0	10.0	30.0	60.0	70.0	60.0	60.0	40.0	0.0	0.0	20.0	0.0	40.0	60.0	60.0	70.0
Poland	8	0.0	0.0	37.5	87.5	25.0	12.5	25.0	37.5	12.5	12.5	25.0	62.5	50.0	37.5	37.5	62.5
Portugal	15	6.7	6.7	46.7	80.0	73.3	40.0	26.7	13.3	0.0	6.7	33.3	40.0	33.3	26.7	53.3	53.3
Romania	4	0.0	0.0	0.0	75.0	75.0	50.0	50.0	50.0	0.0	0.0	0.0	0.0	75.0	25.0	50.0	50.0
Spain	83	6.0	6.0	22.9	80.7	56.6	43.4	32.5	30.1	6.0	8.4	14.5	42.2	25.3	28.9	41.0	61.4
Sweden	18	16.7	22.2	44.4	83.3	72.2	50.0	38.9	44.4	5.6	0.0	0.0	0.0	72.2	38.9	55.6	83.3
Switzerland	15	0.0	6.7	33.3	86.7	53.3	60.0	46.7	33.3	13.3	6.7	20.0	53.3	40.0	40.0	40.0	60.0
Turkey	27	37.0	29.6	37.0	77.8	63.0	33.3	46.7	22.2	7.4	14.8	29.6	51.9	51.9	33.3	22.2	37.0
UK & Ireland	67	17.9	16.4	41.8	89.6	74.6	49.3	25.4	20.9	1.5	3.0	13.4	41.8	62.7	53.7	62.7	64.2
Overall Average	672	10.3	10.6	29.8	80.2	63.2	45.7	28.1	25.1	5.5	8.0	21.3	35.3	45.2	38.2	44.6	58.5

Note that only CAEs responded to this question.

Country	Conflict resolution				Critical thinking				Conceptual thinking				Foreign language skills			
	Audit staff	Senior	Mgr	CAE	Audit staff	Senior	Mgr	CAE	Audit staff	Senior	Mgr	CAE	Audit staff	Senior	Mgr	CAE
Austria	17.4	30.4	37.0	56.5	67.4	37.0	17.4	17.4	28.3	21.7	15.2	39.1	10.9	4.3	2.2	4.3
Belgium	0.0	21.1	26.3	36.8	57.9	42.1	36.8	47.4	10.5	21.1	15.8	31.6	26.3	10.5	10.5	21.1
Bulgaria	19.0	9.5	52.4	66.7	28.6	19.0	47.6	66.7	14.3	14.3	42.9	71.4	42.9	33.3	38.1	66.7
Cyprus	0.0	0.0	33.3	16.7	50.0	33.3	33.3	66.7	16.7	0.0	0.0	0.0	0.0	0.0	0.0	0.0
Czech Republic	20.3	23.7	39.0	50.8	30.5	35.6	16.9	15.3	13.6	18.6	35.6	61.0	20.3	10.2	15.3	25.4
Estonia	16.7	16.7	33.3	66.7	66.7	33.3	0.0	33.3	33.3	16.7	0.0	66.7	33.3	0.0	16.7	50.0
Finland	7.7	7.7	23.1	15.4	30.8	23.1	30.8	53.8	15.4	7.7	7.7	0.0	0.0	0.0	0.0	15.4
France	5.4	18.9	33.8	43.2	39.2	37.8	25.7	21.6	14.9	13.5	25.7	33.8	33.8	20.3	17.6	20.3
Germany	5.6	16.7	27.8	41.7	47.2	33.3	22.2	27.8	22.2	25.0	27.8	38.9	30.6	16.7	16.7	19.4
Greece	0.0	8.3	33.3	66.7	50.0	33.3	41.7	8.3	16.7	0.0	8.3	33.3	0.0	0.0	0.0	8.3
Italy	10.3	20.6	43.9	57.9	53.3	40.2	31.8	38.3	39.3	33.6	36.4	30.8	28.0	17.8	28.0	32.7
Netherlands	7.7	3.8	11.5	19.2	53.8	38.5	15.4	19.2	15.4	15.4	34.6	65.4	15.4	11.5	7.7	7.7
Norway	0.0	10.0	0.0	0.0	60.0	30.0	30.0	20.0	20.0	10.0	0.0	30.0	30.0	20.0	20.0	20.0
Poland	12.5	25.0	50.0	75.0	25.0	25.0	37.5	75.0	12.5	12.5	50.0	75.0	25.0	12.5	37.5	62.5
Portugal	6.7	20.0	53.3	46.7	80.0	60.0	33.3	46.7	20.0	20.0	20.0	6.7	13.3	13.3	20.0	13.3
Romania	25.0	25.0	25.0	50.0	50.0	50.0	25.0	0.0	0.0	50.0	0.0	75.0	75.0	25.0	50.0	50.0
Spain	6.0	26.5	32.5	51.8	47.0	30.1	24.1	24.1	26.5	13.3	12.0	31.3	25.3	24.1	24.1	19.3
Sweden	0.0	16.7	5.6	16.7	61.1	38.9	27.8	27.8	5.6	0.0	0.0	16.7	0.0	0.0	11.1	5.6
Switzerland	6.7	33.3	33.3	53.3	66.7	53.3	53.3	20.0	6.7	20.0	26.7	46.7	53.3	20.0	20.0	26.7
Turkey	7.4	22.2	40.7	48.1	29.6	25.9	11.1	29.6	29.6	22.2	25.9	25.9	22.2	14.8	14.8	29.6
UK & Ireland	1.5	11.9	35.8	35.8	31.3	17.9	23.9	25.4	6.0	7.5	13.4	40.3	3.0	0.0	1.5	1.5
Overall Average	8.5	19.5	34.7	46.4	46.3	34.1	26.0	28.9	20.8	18.0	23.2	37.9	22.3	13.8	16.7	21.0

Note that only CAEs responded to this question.

119

Country	Keeping up to date with professional changes in opinions, standards and regulations				Organization skills				Presentation skills				Problem identification and solution			
	Audit staff	Senior	Mgr	CAE	Audit staff	Senior	Mgr	CAE	Audit staff	Senior	Mgr	CAE	Audit staff	Senior	Mgr	CAE
Austria	43.5	37.0	30.4	34.8	15.2	30.4	30.4	30.4	2.2	15.2	13.0	17.4	41.3	23.9	8.7	17.4
Belgium	5.3	5.3	15.8	52.6	15.8	15.8	36.8	26.3	10.5	10.5	36.8	31.6	47.4	31.6	21.1	10.5
Bulgaria	38.1	28.6	42.9	71.4	4.8	9.5	47.6	71.4	14.3	33.3	42.9	66.7	28.6	33.3	52.4	66.7
Cyprus	0.0	16.7	0.0	16.7	16.7	33.3	16.7	66.7	0.0	0.0	16.7	33.3	66.7	33.3	66.7	33.3
Czech Republic	40.7	39.0	30.5	28.8	8.5	15.3	45.8	50.8	27.1	11.9	28.8	39.0	52.5	39.0	13.6	20.3
Estonia	16.7	16.7	0.0	50.0	16.7	0.0	0.0	50.0	16.7	0.0	16.7	16.7	50.0	16.7	16.7	33.3
Finland	15.4	7.7	23.1	23.1	0.0	0.0	7.7	23.1	15.4	15.4	15.4	38.5	46.2	46.2	15.4	23.1
France	14.9	17.6	21.6	39.2	10.8	24.3	27.0	45.9	24.3	28.4	14.9	28.4	47.3	32.4	18.9	17.6
Germany	22.2	19.4	19.4	11.1	16.7	25.0	16.7	33.3	8.3	27.8	16.7	8.3	47.2	27.8	11.1	19.4
Greece	0.0	0.0	33.3	33.3	8.3	16.7	25.0	33.3	8.3	33.3	16.7	33.3	33.3	16.7	33.3	16.7
Italy	32.7	37.4	42.1	45.8	8.4	21.5	35.5	53.3	13.1	18.7	35.5	41.1	32.7	32.7	47.7	43.0
Netherlands	15.4	19.2	26.9	19.2	3.8	7.7	26.9	46.2	11.5	15.4	11.5	26.9	34.6	38.5	23.1	7.7
Norway	10.0	10.0	30.0	20.0	0.0	10.0	10.0	40.0	30.0	30.0	40.0	70.0	40.0	20.0	30.0	20.0
Poland	50.0	37.5	25.0	62.5	0.0	25.0	50.0	75.0	12.5	12.5	37.5	87.5	37.5	37.5	50.0	75.0
Portugal	20.0	26.7	53.3	53.3	33.3	20.0	40.0	46.7	6.7	6.7	20.0	26.7	40.0	60.0	26.7	33.3
Romania	25.0	25.0	75.0	25.0	0.0	0.0	75.0	25.0	25.0	25.0	0.0	25.0	50.0	50.0	25.0	0.0
Spain	44.6	42.2	41.0	44.6	14.5	18.1	27.7	36.1	10.8	14.5	21.7	20.5	33.7	32.5	26.5	37.3
Sweden	22.2	5.6	11.1	33.3	5.6	11.1	16.7	16.7	22.2	0.0	11.1	38.9	55.6	22.2	16.7	22.2
Switzerland	40.0	33.3	33.3	40.0	13.3	26.7	13.3	26.7	0.0	13.3	26.7	26.7	60.0	26.7	20.0	13.3
Turkey	48.1	40.7	18.5	22.2	14.8	22.2	33.3	33.3	18.5	18.5	11.1	33.3	51.9	33.3	25.9	33.3
UK & Ireland	11.9	11.9	22.4	29.9	13.4	20.9	32.8	19.4	13.4	16.4	26.9	38.8	49.3	41.8	23.9	17.9
Overall Average	28.4	27.4	30.2	36.8	11.3	19.5	30.8	40.2	14.4	17.9	23.5	32.7	42.7	33.5	26.2	27.4

Note that only CAEs responded to this question.

Country	Project planning and management				Report management				Time management				Training and developing staff			
	Audit staff	Senior	Mgr	CAE	Audit staff	Senior	Mgr	CAE	Audit staff	Senior	Mgr	CAE	Audit staff	Senior	Mgr	CAE
Austria	6.5	17.4	21.7	13.0	4.3	6.5	8.7	2.2	26.1	23.9	8.7	8.7	2.2	6.5	32.6	45.7
Belgium	0.0	31.6	26.3	10.5	21.1	31.6	10.5	5.3	26.3	21.1	15.8	15.8	0.0	26.3	52.6	21.1
Bulgaria	9.5	14.3	52.4	61.9	19.0	23.8	38.1	61.9	38.1	38.1	42.9	61.9	23.8	28.6	47.6	71.4
Cyprus	0.0	0.0	16.7	16.7	16.7	33.3	50.0	16.7	66.7	50.0	33.3	50.0	0.0	16.7	33.3	16.7
Czech Republic	5.1	3.4	37.3	28.8	18.6	22.0	13.6	5.1	5.1	16.9	23.7	25.4	0.0	10.2	30.5	33.9
Estonia	16.7	16.7	50.0	33.3	50.0	16.7	16.7	16.7	33.3	16.7	16.7	16.7	0.0	0.0	0.0	33.3
Finland	23.1	7.7	30.8	7.7	7.7	15.4	0.0	0.0	7.7	0.0	0.0	0.0	0.0	0.0	0.0	15.4
France	5.4	23.0	24.3	21.6	39.2	35.1	12.2	13.5	31.1	27.0	13.5	13.5	2.7	4.1	23.0	29.7
Germany	5.6	25.0	16.7	13.9	2.8	19.4	16.7	2.8	25.0	16.7	13.9	5.6	0.0	8.3	19.4	16.7
Greece	0.0	8.3	25.0	33.3	0.0	16.7	41.7	16.7	58.3	41.7	33.3	33.3	0.0	41.7	16.7	33.3
Italy	6.5	21.5	44.9	39.3	29.9	40.2	40.2	27.1	34.6	35.5	33.6	30.8	5.6	14.0	32.7	45.8
Netherlands	7.7	19.2	23.1	11.5	15.4	11.5	19.2	0.0	38.5	19.2	3.8	11.5	0.0	15.4	30.8	11.5
Norway	10.0	0.0	40.0	10.0	30.0	20.0	0.0	0.0	10.0	10.0	0.0	0.0	0.0	20.0	0.0	40.0
Poland	0.0	37.5	37.5	25.0	25.0	12.5	25.0	62.5	25.0	25.0	37.5	87.5	0.0	12.5	25.0	50.0
Portugal	0.0	33.3	53.3	33.3	46.7	33.3	20.0	13.3	46.7	20.0	26.7	20.0	13.3	20.0	26.7	13.3
Romania	0.0	25.0	25.0	50.0	50.0	50.0	25.0	0.0	25.0	25.0	0.0	0.0	0.0	0.0	50.0	75.0
Spain	6.0	12.0	34.9	27.7	39.8	34.9	26.5	18.1	36.1	31.3	21.7	15.7	1.2	19.3	34.9	38.6
Sweden	0.0	16.7	16.7	11.1	22.2	16.7	5.6	11.1	16.7	5.6	5.6	0.0	0.0	11.1	16.7	38.9
Switzerland	0.0	40.0	13.3	13.3	6.7	13.3	13.3	6.7	33.3	40.0	13.3	13.3	6.7	13.3	33.3	6.7
Turkey	7.4	22.2	37.0	33.3	44.4	22.2	14.8	18.5	33.3	29.6	22.2	25.9	7.4	29.6	37.0	37.0
UK & Ireland	10.4	26.9	37.3	23.9	23.9	25.4	17.9	7.5	58.2	32.8	10.4	4.5	0.0	20.9	52.2	25.4
Overall Average	6.3	19.0	33.0	25.9	25.6	26.8	21.0	14.4	32.4	26.9	19.3	18.8	3.0	14.7	31.8	34.1

Note that only CAEs responded to this question.

Country	Understanding complex information systems				Writing skills			
	Audit staff	Senior	Mgr	CAE	Audit staff	Senior	Mgr	CAE
Austria	21.7	15.2	4.3	2.2	43.5	19.6	13.0	17.4
Belgium	15.8	15.8	10.5	5.3	57.9	31.6	15.8	10.5
Bulgaria	23.8	38.1	33.3	52.4	52.4	28.6	42.9	66.7
Cyprus	0.0	0.0	0.0	16.7	33.3	50.0	0.0	0.0
Czech Republic	25.4	22.0	15.3	16.9	64.4	15.3	15.3	11.9
Estonia	0.0	0.0	0.0	16.7	66.7	16.7	0.0	33.3
Finland	7.7	0.0	0.0	7.7	23.1	23.1	7.7	23.1
France	23.0	14.9	8.1	8.1	48.6	24.3	9.5	17.6
Germany	27.8	25.0	5.6	5.6	38.9	22.2	8.3	8.3
Greece	16.7	16.7	0.0	16.7	58.3	41.7	25.0	16.7
Italy	16.8	20.6	25.2	19.6	39.3	25.2	28.0	25.2
Netherlands	23.1	19.2	15.4	7.7	50.0	46.2	15.4	11.5
Norway	40.0	10.0	20.0	20.0	50.0	50.0	60.0	40.0
Poland	12.5	12.5	25.0	37.5	50.0	25.0	25.0	87.5
Portugal	26.7	26.7	33.3	20.0	53.3	53.3	20.0	13.3
Romania	0.0	25.0	25.0	0.0	25.0	25.0	0.0	0.0
Spain	22.9	24.1	13.3	9.6	45.8	25.3	16.9	13.3
Sweden	16.7	0.0	0.0	0.0	33.3	0.0	5.6	5.6
Switzerland	46.7	26.7	13.3	6.7	33.3	40.0	20.0	20.0
Turkey	37.0	22.2	7.4	22.2	40.7	11.1	7.4	22.2
UK & Ireland	11.9	14.9	14.9	6.0	58.2	35.8	26.9	22.4
Overall Average	**21.3**	**18.9**	**14.0**	**12.8**	**47.3**	**26.3**	**18.5**	**19.8**

Note that only CAEs responded to this question.

7.5. Knowledge Areas

Table 55 shows the knowledge areas that respondents consider most important for internal audit practitioners. The seven most important knowledge areas are:

- Auditing (average score of 4.58) except in Austria, France and Germany;
- Internal auditing standards (average score of 4.02) except in France, Germany and Norway;
- Ethics (average score of 3.95) except in Austria, France and Germany;
- Enterprise risk management (average score of 3.84) expect in Austria, Germany and Greece;

- Technical knowledge for your industry (average score of 3.79) except in Austria, Germany and Netherlands;
- Governance (average score of 3.76) except in Austria, Germany and Netherlands;
- Information technology (average score of 3.76) except in Belgium, Estonia and France.

Table 55: Knowledge Areas (means)

Country	Total Number of Respondents	Accounting	Auditing	Business law and government regulations	Business management	Changes to professional standards	Enterprise Risk Management	Ethics	Finance	Fraud awareness	Governance
Austria	28	4.04	4.11	3.75	3.18	3.04	3.46	3.39	3.39	4.14	3.46
Belgium	64	3.41	4.61	3.43	3.43	3.38	3.98	4.03	3.61	3.59	3.71
Bulgaria	29	3.93	4.57	3.64	3.53	4.10	3.90	4.07	4.18	3.93	3.73
Cyprus	18	4.22	4.50	3.83	3.89	4.00	4.28	3.94	3.88	4.00	4.00
Czech Republic	82	3.60	4.65	3.37	3.48	3.41	3.83	3.80	3.82	3.63	3.92
Estonia	5	2.80	4.80	3.20	3.60	3.20	3.60	4.00	3.20	4.00	4.00
Finland	26	4.00	4.46	3.88	3.69	3.35	3.96	4.23	3.81	3.81	4.23
France	135	3.16	4.45	2.96	2.95	2.99	3.95	3.53	3.28	3.53	3.30
Germany	64	3.50	4.05	3.47	3.51	3.11	3.68	3.32	2.97	3.67	3.32
Greece	49	3.90	4.57	3.76	3.50	3.16	3.63	3.96	3.71	4.08	3.78
Italy	237	3.52	4.62	3.94	3.54	3.61	3.80	4.06	3.45	3.72	3.90
Netherlands	67	3.49	4.61	3.51	3.62	3.57	3.94	3.88	3.52	3.45	3.84
Norway	21	3.14	4.67	3.71	4.10	3.76	4.25	4.19	3.38	3.67	3.95
Poland	56	3.88	4.69	4.11	3.77	3.57	4.02	4.11	4.26	3.84	3.35
Portugal	81	3.73	4.64	3.75	3.56	3.88	3.72	4.37	3.66	3.91	3.70
Romania	23	3.87	4.78	4.22	4.04	4.26	4.26	4.74	4.00	4.00	4.04
Spain	125	3.96	4.62	3.76	3.78	3.73	3.94	4.17	3.86	3.89	3.80
Sweden	35	3.46	4.57	4.06	3.54	3.00	3.83	4.14	3.06	3.29	3.69
Switzerland	17	3.53	4.71	3.71	3.71	3.82	4.18	4.06	3.59	3.65	3.63
Turkey	35	4.46	4.83	3.89	3.54	3.89	3.83	4.34	4.17	4.20	3.85
UK & Ireland	158	3.03	4.68	3.46	3.54	3.45	3.61	3.73	3.52	3.64	4.08
Overall Average	**1,356**	**3.56**	**4.58**	**3.64**	**3.52**	**3.50**	**3.84**	**3.95**	**3.59**	**3.73**	**3.76**

Note that CAEs did <u>not</u> answer this question.
Ranking from 1 (minimally important) to 5 (very important).

Country	Human resource management	Internal auditing standards	Information technology	Managerial accounting	Marketing	Organization culture	Organizational systems	Strategy and business policy	Technical knowledge for your industry
Austria	3.30	3.96	3.93	3.48	2.59	3.54	3.75	3.68	3.25
Belgium	2.94	3.89	3.45	3.03	2.24	3.70	3.80	3.48	3.60
Bulgaria	3.50	4.43	4.03	3.79	3.13	3.80	3.57	3.63	4.00
Cyprus	3.94	4.18	3.83	3.44	3.22	4.00	4.00	3.94	3.94
Czech Republic	3.18	4.17	3.69	3.24	2.67	3.29	3.60	2.95	3.93
Estonia	3.00	4.80	3.20	3.60	2.20	4.00	4.00	4.40	3.40
Finland	3.19	4.31	4.19	3.65	2.65	3.42	3.42	3.81	3.62
France	2.92	3.58	3.45	3.16	2.18	3.70	3.61	3.00	3.79
Germany	3.06	3.75	3.72	3.24	2.53	3.41	3.63	3.52	3.13
Greece	3.35	3.92	3.71	3.48	2.63	3.78	3.83	3.73	3.84
Italy	3.42	4.00	3.59	3.22	2.66	3.76	3.61	3.36	4.16
Netherlands	3.00	3.89	3.94	3.17	2.11	3.65	3.67	3.40	3.31
Norway	3.05	3.76	4.00	2.95	2.15	3.76	3.67	4.00	3.45
Poland	3.51	4.43	3.73	3.45	2.57	3.57	3.75	3.36	3.33
Portugal	3.36	4.43	4.23	3.53	2.79	3.86	3.75	3.68	3.84
Romania	4.00	4.61	4.04	3.74	3.48	4.00	4.17	4.09	3.74
Spain	3.37	4.10	3.85	3.57	2.73	3.98	3.54	3.64	3.96
Sweden	3.11	3.86	3.76	3.11	2.17	4.23	4.03	3.91	3.40
Switzerland	3.24	4.19	4.00	3.35	2.65	3.59	3.76	3.71	3.82
Turkey	3.43	4.12	3.94	3.80	3.09	4.09	3.91	3.74	3.77
UK & Ireland	3.17	3.97	3.84	2.96	2.39	3.92	3.90	3.89	3.90
Overall Average	**3.25**	**4.02**	**3.76**	**3.29**	**2.56**	**3.75**	**3.71**	**3.52**	**3.79**

Note that CAEs did <u>not</u> answer this question.
Ranking from 1 (minimally important) to 5 (very important).

8 Emerging Issues

In the eight and last section of the questionnaire, all respondents were asked to indicate how they expect their internal audit function is going to evolve in the next three years.

8.1. Evolution in the Status of the Internal Audit Function

Respondents (excluding CAEs) were asked to indicate whether the following statements currently apply or are likely to apply within the next three years to their organization:

a. Internal auditing is required by law or regulation where the organization is based.
b. Internal auditors in the organization have an advisory role in strategy development.
c. The organization complies with a corporate governance code.
d. The organization has implemented an internal control framework.
e. The organization has implemented a knowledge management system.
f. The Internal Audit Function has provided training to audit committee members.
g. The Internal Audit Function assumes an important role in the integrity of financial reporting.
h. The Internal Audit Function educates organization personnel about internal controls, corporate governance, and compliance issues.
i. The Internal Audit Function places more emphasis on assurance than consulting services.

Table 56 shows that an IAF is mandatory in 64% of the cases. Some 14% expect this to happen in the next 3 years. IAF's are only in 24% of the cases involved in strategy development. In 95% of the cases, control frameworks will be implemented within the next 3 years. Training to audit committee members and organizational personnel is strongly on the rise. Providing assurance rather than consulting still remains the core business.

Table 56: Evolution in the Status of the Internal Audit Function (%)

Country	Total Number of Respondents	a		b		c		d	
		Currently Apply	Likely to apply in the next 3 years	Currently Apply	Likely to apply in the next 3 years	Currently Apply	Likely to apply in the next 3 years	Currently Apply	Likely to apply in the next 3 years
Austria	70	68.6	12.9	25.7	28.6	36.2	34.8	57.4	25.7
Belgium	78	59.0	6.4	11.7	39.0	61.5	24.4	67.9	11.7
Bulgaria	53	64.2	15.1	26.4	50.9	35.8	37.7	61.5	26.4
Cyprus	25	52.0	28.0	28.0	40.0	62.5	20.8	60.0	28.0
Czech Republic	140	72.1	9.3	24.6	37.0	53.3	29.9	48.6	24.6
Estonia	10	70.0	0.0	60.0	10.0	50.0	50.0	60.0	60.0
Finland	35	28.6	22.9	23.5	23.5	48.6	42.9	48.6	23.5
France	195	55.4	17.4	21.4	25.0	58.2	23.0	82.6	21.4
Germany	89	50.6	21.3	15.7	22.5	47.7	29.1	44.3	15.7
Greece	60	76.7	10.0	20.0	41.7	68.3	23.3	71.7	20.0
Italy	334	68.0	16.2	28.2	34.5	72.7	18.2	80.2	28.2
Netherlands	89	73.0	9.0	16.1	21.8	67.4	22.5	74.7	16.1
Norway	30	53.3	13.3	23.3	10.0	67.7	16.1	64.5	23.3
Poland	61	80.3	9.8	36.1	44.3	38.7	33.9	80.6	36.1
Portugal	91	52.7	16.5	25.6	40.0	59.8	25.3	81.3	25.6
Romania	27	85.2	14.8	40.7	51.9	59.3	25.9	66.7	40.7
Spain	204	63.2	16.2	23.6	33.5	67.6	22.2	72.8	23.6
Sweden	52	75.0	9.6	17.3	34.6	42.3	13.5	48.1	17.3
Switzerland	32	56.3	12.5	6.3	25.0	65.6	28.1	45.2	6.3
Turkey	58	51.7	36.2	27.6	46.6	58.6	32.8	63.2	27.6
UK & Ireland	218	69.3	8.3	26.4	26.8	85.5	9.1	82.7	26.4
Overall Average	**1,951**	**64.2**	**14.4**	**24.0**	**32.6**	**62.6**	**23.1**	**70.6**	**24.0**

Note that this question was <u>not</u> answered by CAEs
and that the answering categories are mutually exclusive.

Country	e		f		g		h		i	
	Currently Apply	Likely to apply in the next 3 years	Currently Apply	Likely to apply in the next 3 years	Currently Apply	Likely to apply in the next 3 years	Currently Apply	Likely to apply in the next 3 years	Currently Apply	Likely to apply in the next 3 years
Austria	11.6	44.9	1.5	11.9	29.4	30.9	17.6	33.8	73.9	14.5
Belgium	27.8	40.5	33.8	27.3	45.6	32.9	55.1	25.6	70.9	19.0
Bulgaria	26.4	50.9	13.2	43.4	32.7	46.2	45.3	34.0	64.2	30.2
Cyprus	12.0	52.0	28.0	36.0	60.0	24.0	48.0	40.0	48.0	28.0
Czech Republic	31.6	40.4	13.3	22.2	22.6	35.0	51.1	30.9	73.9	13.8
Estonia	30.0	60.0	11.1	33.3	20.0	30.0	80.0	20.0	70.0	10.0
Finland	35.3	38.2	25.7	28.6	35.3	23.5	45.7	40.0	42.9	34.3
France	30.2	32.3	22.6	27.2	39.9	25.4	47.2	32.1	66.3	12.4
Germany	32.6	28.1	9.1	15.9	38.6	26.1	29.2	29.2	69.7	9.0
Greece	37.9	44.8	35.0	33.3	43.1	32.8	46.6	43.1	62.7	18.6
Italy	26.7	47.9	22.4	37.7	37.4	37.4	57.8	30.3	65.7	18.3
Netherlands	21.3	41.6	13.5	41.6	67.4	20.2	45.5	29.5	78.7	13.5
Norway	35.5	38.7	40.0	26.7	50.0	16.7	63.3	26.7	76.7	16.7
Poland	14.5	46.8	16.4	14.8	24.2	32.3	45.2	40.3	71.0	16.1
Portugal	32.2	44.8	19.3	23.9	39.3	28.1	55.6	25.6	70.5	13.6
Romania	37.0	59.3	29.6	44.4	48.1	29.6	48.1	51.9	74.1	25.9
Spain	31.1	47.6	28.4	33.3	61.1	24.1	57.6	28.1	68.5	13.3
Sweden	25.5	37.3	15.4	25.0	34.6	19.2	31.4	27.5	64.7	13.7
Switzerland	22.6	48.4	18.8	28.1	53.1	12.5	40.6	25.0	78.1	9.4
Turkey	55.2	36.2	17.5	36.8	50.9	35.1	34.5	51.7	56.4	30.9
UK & Ireland	26.9	44.4	45.6	26.0	65.1	17.9	68.3	18.1	87.1	5.5
Overall Average	**28.6**	**42.9**	**23.6**	**29.5**	**44.5**	**28.4**	**50.9**	**30.3**	**70.2**	**15.3**

Note that this question was <u>not</u> answered by CAEs
and that the answering categories are mutually exclusive

Comparing all 21 European countries, we notice:

- a high percentage for a **requirement by law or regulation to have internal auditing (currently apply and likely to apply in the next 3 years)** in Greece, Poland, Romania and Turkey;
- a high percentage for **internal auditors to have an advisory role in strategy development (currently apply and likely to apply in the next 3 years)** in Bulgaria, Poland, Romania and Turkey;
- a high percentage for **organizations complying with corporate governance codes** in Estonia, Greece, Switzerland and UK & Ireland;
- a high percentage for **organizations implementing a knowledge management system** in Bulgaria, Estonia, Greece and Romania;
- a high percentage for **IAFs Providing training to Audit Committee members** in Greece, Norway, Romania and UK & Ireland;
- a high percentage of **IAFs assuming a role in the integrity of financial reporting** in Cyprus, Spain, Turkey and UK & Ireland;
- a high percentage of **IAFs educating personnel about internal controls, corporate governance, and compliance issues** in Estonia, Greece, Norway and Romania;
- a high percentage of **IAFs placing more emphasis on assurance than consulting services** in Netherlands, Norway, Romania and UK & Ireland.

8.2.   Changes in the Role of the Internal Audit Function

Table 57 shows that all five areas are on the rise with risk management in the lead with over 81% of the respondents expecting an increase in the next three years, and governance on the second place with 64% expecting an increase. The largest decrease is expected in the area of reviewing financial processes (20%).

A comparison of all 21 countries reveals:

- a high expected increase in the role of the IAF in **reviewing financial processes** in Bulgaria, Poland, Portugal, Romania and Turkey;
- a high expected increase in the role of the IAF in **risk management** in Austria, Portugal, Romania and Turkey;
- a high expected increase in the role of the IAF in **governance** in Romania, Sweden, Turkey and UK & Ireland,
- a high expected increase in the role of the IAF in **regulatory compliance** is in Cyprus, Netherlands, Portugal and Switzerland;
- a high expected increase in the role of the IAF in **operational auditing** in Bulgaria, Portugal, Romania and Turkey.

Table 57: Changes in the Role of the Internal Audit Function over the Next 3 Years (part 1) (%)

Country	Total Number of Respondents	Review of financial processes		Risk management		Governance		Regulatory compliance		Operational auditing	
		Increase	Decrease	Increase	Decrease	Increase	Decrease	Increase	Decrease	Increase	Decrease
Austria	73	35.6	9.6	90.4	0.0	62.5	2.8	46.6	9.6	52.1	5.5
Belgium	80	36.3	12.5	70.7	4.9	61.7	7.4	35.4	8.9	41.5	24.4
Bulgaria	52	57.7	5.8	86.5	1.9	48.1	7.7	47.1	5.9	57.7	9.6
Cyprus	25	48.0	12.0	88.0	0.0	60.0	0.0	52.0	4.0	48.0	4.0
Czech Republic	140	38.6	46.4	74.8	18.7	55.4	35.3	38.8	47.5	30.1	55.9
Estonia	10	10.0	40.0	70.0	0.0	40.0	0.0	40.0	20.0	20.0	0.0
Finland	38	39.5	15.8	76.3	5.3	39.5	5.3	24.3	18.9	21.6	8.1
France	196	38.3	11.2	72.0	2.0	48.2	3.0	33.8	15.7	33.3	14.1
Germany	96	43.8	11.5	76.0	2.1	64.2	2.1	32.6	12.6	47.4	6.3
Greece	62	41.9	8.1	87.1	1.6	59.7	0.0	48.4	1.6	44.3	13.1
Italy	345	41.7	19.7	84.6	2.3	70.6	3.5	51.0	11.5	41.5	13.8
Netherlands	92	31.5	35.9	72.8	2.2	68.5	3.3	57.1	8.8	50.5	19.8
Norway	31	41.9	16.1	77.4	3.2	48.4	6.5	20.0	6.7	32.3	22.6
Poland	64	48.4	10.9	85.7	4.8	63.5	1.6	25.4	19.0	46.0	11.1
Portugal	92	51.1	14.1	89.1	0.0	64.5	3.2	60.9	10.9	52.2	18.9
Romania	27	51.9	22.2	96.0	0.0	77.8	0.0	40.7	44.4	55.6	11.1
Spain	210	27.6	23.8	85.7	1.0	68.9	1.9	50.7	5.3	35.9	14.4
Sweden	53	35.8	22.6	81.1	0.0	71.2	1.9	25.0	30.8	32.1	15.1
Switzerland	32	28.1	15.6	75.0	0.0	61.3	0.0	62.5	9.4	21.9	21.9
Turkey	61	55.7	14.8	90.0	0.0	78.3	5.0	50.0	18.3	55.7	13.1
UK & Ireland	228	32.9	21.9	82.4	2.6	72.7	1.3	36.3	16.4	28.6	25.1
Overall Average	**2,007**	**39.0**	**19.6**	**81.4**	**3.1**	**63.9**	**5.1**	**43.2**	**15.0**	**39.6**	**18.1**

Table 58: Changes in the Role of the Internal Audit Function
over the Next 3 years (part 2) (%)

Country	Total Number of Respondents	Alignment of strategy and performance measures		Benchmarking		Corporate governance		Corporate social responsibility	
		Currently have a role	Likely to have a role in the next 3 years	Currently have a role	Likely to have a role in the next 3 years	Currently have a role	Likely to have a role in the next 3 years	Currently have a role	Likely to have a role in the next 3 years
Austria	69	8.7	24.6	24.6	36.2	19.7	36.4	3.2	17.7
Belgium	79	17.7	32.9	17.5	40.0	51.9	35.4	14.5	43.4
Bulgaria	51	5.9	66.7	27.5	58.8	25.5	43.1	26.0	34.0
Cyprus	25	16.0	32.0	28.0	40.0	48.0	36.0	24.0	36.0
Czech Republic	139	16.5	48.2	24.5	49.6	40.1	38.0	11.9	25.2
Estonia	10	30.0	50.0	40.0	10.0	50.0	30.0	11.1	33.3
Finland	36	33.3	16.7	33.3	25.0	51.4	34.3	8.6	48.6
France	194	22.2	30.9	27.3	34.0	44.3	39.2	16.2	33.0
Germany	89	11.2	22.5	28.7	28.7	33.0	37.5	5.7	23.0
Greece	59	15.3	39.0	28.8	35.6	60.0	30.0	26.7	33.3
Italy	331	15.7	41.7	29.0	34.7	66.7	25.0	24.8	39.7
Netherlands	90	27.8	26.7	24.4	31.1	68.1	28.6	18.9	35.6
Norway	30	23.3	16.7	24.1	20.7	70.0	23.3	17.2	34.5
Poland	60	6.7	33.3	15.0	31.7	22.0	40.7	3.4	15.3
Portugal	89	19.1	38.2	27.1	35.3	38.1	36.9	34.1	32.9
Romania	26	46.2	38.5	32.0	52.0	36.0	64.0	24.0	68.0
Spain	202	33.7	36.6	20.3	34.2	39.2	44.6	20.9	48.8
Sweden	51	19.6	21.6	36.5	26.9	28.8	26.9	19.2	19.2
Switzerland	32	12.5	18.8	12.9	32.3	62.5	25.0	12.5	9.4
Turkey	58	15.5	48.3	33.9	41.1	43.1	48.3	30.9	38.2
UK & Ireland	219	25.1	34.7	30.7	27.1	79.5	14.3	25.5	32.7
Overall Average	**1,939**	**20.1**	**35.7**	**26.6**	**34.9**	**50.9**	**32.9**	**19.6**	**34.5**

Country	Develop training and education of organization personnel		Disaster recovery		Evidential issues		Emerging markets		Environmental sustainability	
	Currently have a role	Likely to have a role in the next 3 years	Currently have a role	Likely to have a role in the next 3 years	Currently have a role	Likely to have a role in the next 3 years	Currently have a role	Likely to have a role in the next 3 years	Currently have a role	Likely to have a role in the next 3 years
Austria	10.4	40.3	14.7	23.5	50.0	22.1	11.6	13.0	3.0	18.2
Belgium	43.2	35.8	28.8	22.5	30.0	16.3	8.9	17.7	8.9	22.8
Bulgaria	37.3	56.9	22.0	34.0	60.0	30.0	9.8	27.5	16.0	30.0
Cyprus	48.0	28.0	32.0	32.0	28.0	48.0	20.0	32.0	20.0	20.0
Czech Republic	45.3	35.8	21.9	27.7	29.9	26.3	6.0	22.4	9.6	16.2
Estonia	50.0	37.5	37.5	37.5	33.3	11.1	12.5	12.5	12.5	12.5
Finland	36.1	52.8	19.4	38.9	28.6	34.3	22.2	16.7	19.4	27.8
France	47.7	29.7	9.5	12.1	22.5	20.9	9.4	21.5	11.6	31.1
Germany	22.2	33.3	18.4	20.7	43.3	23.3	12.8	15.1	6.7	18.0
Greece	39.0	45.8	28.8	42.4	34.5	36.2	17.5	28.1	12.1	37.9
Italy	52.5	32.2	26.3	26.9	27.8	25.6	12.2	20.1	11.7	28.6
Netherlands	38.9	32.2	25.8	18.0	25.3	20.7	6.9	16.1	15.6	25.6
Norway	26.7	60.0	36.7	6.7	23.3	13.3	10.3	13.8	10.3	13.8
Poland	29.3	53.4	1.7	5.2	30.5	13.6	.0	5.1	.0	15.5
Portugal	47.1	33.3	28.2	27.1	60.9	13.8	17.0	22.7	27.9	18.6
Romania	61.5	38.5	15.4	53.8	41.7	45.8	8.0	60.0	16.0	56.0
Spain	52.0	33.3	15.3	20.8	49.0	18.9	9.3	22.1	11.9	30.7
Sweden	29.4	31.4	7.8	7.8	23.1	11.5	11.5	9.6	25.0	17.3
Switzerland	31.3	37.5	9.4	12.5	29.0	16.1	9.4	18.8	3.1	12.5
Turkey	40.4	45.6	20.7	46.6	45.6	28.1	8.6	32.8	10.7	33.9
UK & Ireland	46.2	29.1	47.7	18.0	38.6	15.7	8.3	16.7	13.6	27.1
Overall Average	**43.2**	**35.5**	**23.3**	**23.1**	**35.6**	**22.0**	**10.3**	**20.1**	**12.3**	**25.8**

Country	Executive compensation		Fraud prevention / detection		Globalization		Intellectual property and knowledge assessment		IT management assessment	
	Currently have a role	Likely to have a role in the next 3 years	Currently have a role	Likely to have a role in the next 3 years	Currently have a role	Likely to have a role in the next 3 years	Currently have a role	Likely to have a role in the next 3 years	Currently have a role	Likely to have a role in the next 3 years
Austria	0.0	4.4	70.8	25.0	3.0	13.4	8.8	7.4	31.4	40.0
Belgium	8.9	16.5	62.5	27.5	15.0	15.0	14.1	26.9	48.1	32.9
Bulgaria	20.0	24.0	54.9	39.2	13.7	39.2	14.0	50.0	38.8	55.1
Cyprus	12.0	20.0	58.3	41.7	16.0	16.0	16.7	25.0	32.0	40.0
Czech Republic	8.9	17.0	46.0	42.4	9.7	23.9	18.9	37.9	38.5	46.7
Estonia	37.5	25.0	77.8	11.1	33.3	0.0	33.3	44.4	44.4	44.4
Finland	16.7	16.7	63.9	25.0	28.6	17.1	28.6	14.3	40.0	31.4
France	13.5	11.9	65.3	23.1	13.0	19.3	16.8	19.9	46.4	36.2
Germany	3.4	3.4	67.8	23.3	13.8	17.2	8.0	14.8	46.1	24.7
Greece	15.3	25.4	69.0	24.1	23.7	23.7	22.8	22.8	35.6	35.6
Italy	8.7	18.1	62.2	26.7	11.2	19.9	15.7	21.5	50.9	29.4
Netherlands	16.1	18.4	60.2	23.9	17.2	23.0	11.6	31.4	47.7	29.1
Norway	26.7	16.7	83.3	13.3	20.0	16.7	6.9	24.1	53.3	13.3
Poland	3.4	12.1	44.1	32.2	11.9	11.9	8.3	26.7	31.7	43.3
Portugal	21.6	12.5	70.8	21.3	23.5	27.1	16.3	27.9	45.9	31.8
Romania	15.4	50.0	53.8	34.6	3.8	65.4	19.2	57.7	34.6	57.7
Spain	12.0	22.0	65.8	19.3	11.9	26.7	10.0	31.3	37.3	38.8
Sweden	19.2	11.5	55.8	21.2	20.0	14.0	28.0	14.0	63.5	26.9
Switzerland	6.3	9.4	59.4	28.1	9.7	6.5	9.4	9.4	56.3	28.1
Turkey	8.6	12.1	81.0	13.8	14.0	21.1	10.5	47.4	46.4	44.6
UK & Ireland	9.6	11.4	73.5	13.2	9.6	9.6	20.8	19.9	50.0	22.5
Overall Average	**11.3**	**15.7**	**64.0**	**24.5**	**13.3**	**20.0**	**15.4**	**25.4**	**44.9**	**33.9**

Country	Knowledge management systems development review		Mergers and acquisitions		Project management		Provide training to the audit committee		Regulatory compliance assessment monitoring	
	Currently have a role	Likely to have a role in the next 3 years	Currently have a role	Likely to have a role in the next 3 years	Currently have a role	Likely to have a role in the next 3 years	Currently have a role	Likely to have a role in the next 3 years	Currently have a role	Likely to have a role in the next 3 years
Austria	9.0	43.3	5.8	21.7	30.4	30.4	1.5	14.7	84.3	12.9
Belgium	36.7	27.8	21.8	16.7	48.7	19.2	31.3	33.8	53.8	22.5
Bulgaria	20.0	58.0	5.8	34.6	32.0	42.0	3.9	54.9	58.0	30.0
Cyprus	24.0	44.0	8.0	16.0	16.0	40.0	20.0	44.0	43.5	47.8
Czech Republic	21.1	43.6	6.7	20.9	30.9	34.6	11.3	29.3	57.0	24.4
Estonia	33.3	44.4	.0	25.0	33.3	55.6	12.5	25.0	75.0	12.5
Finland	20.0	48.6	17.1	22.9	48.6	25.7	22.9	37.1	45.7	28.6
France	16.0	39.2	18.8	20.3	35.0	31.0	24.6	29.2	71.8	21.5
Germany	14.8	37.5	19.3	26.1	38.2	30.3	3.4	17.0	79.8	13.5
Greece	21.8	52.7	24.1	29.3	40.4	31.6	33.9	37.3	56.9	31.0
Italy	17.1	42.5	17.7	29.1	32.8	27.7	22.1	40.8	79.5	14.8
Netherlands	22.4	31.8	27.3	15.9	39.8	23.9	13.5	48.3	50.0	39.5
Norway	33.3	13.3	20.0	26.7	36.7	23.3	33.3	33.3	50.0	30.0
Poland	5.2	46.6	6.7	23.3	23.7	49.2	13.3	21.7	67.2	19.0
Portugal	19.8	38.4	15.1	18.6	31.8	18.8	16.3	29.1	60.5	22.1
Romania	28.0	68.0	26.9	46.2	30.8	53.8	23.1	57.7	57.7	30.8
Spain	16.6	44.2	25.6	23.6	31.2	22.6	39.7	31.9	74.8	15.5
Sweden	23.1	36.5	9.6	9.6	38.5	17.3	17.6	23.5	62.7	9.8
Switzerland	15.6	50.0	12.5	25.0	46.9	34.4	15.6	37.5	81.3	12.5
Turkey	28.1	45.6	15.8	38.6	28.1	38.6	17.9	42.9	66.1	32.1
UK & Ireland	32.7	34.6	17.9	15.1	58.4	18.3	45.0	30.5	56.9	20.6
Overall Average	**20.7**	**40.9**	**17.2**	**23.0**	**37.0**	**28.1**	**23.6**	**33.5**	**66.8**	**20.9**

Country	Risk management		Strategic frameworks	
	Currently have a role	Likely to have a role in the next 3 years	Currently have a role	Likely to have a role in the next 3 years
Austria	44.9	42.0	16.2	27.9
Belgium	70.9	19.0	15.2	35.4
Bulgaria	51.9	40.4	33.3	47.1
Cyprus	56.0	44.0	20.8	45.8
Czech Republic	63.2	30.9	24.6	38.8
Estonia	80.0	20.0	44.4	44.4
Finland	65.7	22.9	31.4	20.0
France	77.4	17.6	17.3	35.1
Germany	66.7	25.6	6.7	33.3
Greece	50.8	42.4	13.6	47.5
Italy	65.6	27.5	15.6	36.2
Netherlands	62.9	31.5	17.0	36.4
Norway	62.1	24.1	13.3	36.7
Poland	55.7	24.6	8.2	45.9
Portugal	51.7	34.8	26.2	35.7
Romania	61.5	38.5	23.1	73.1
Spain	67.0	22.3	24.0	37.7
Sweden	73.1	25.0	43.1	23.5
Switzerland	75.0	15.6	9.4	18.8
Turkey	56.1	38.6	13.2	60.4
UK & Ireland	82.4	12.2	37.9	31.5
Overall Average	**66.3**	**26.0**	**21.3**	**36.8**

Table 58 shows that IAFs are **currently** most active in the following areas:

- Regulatory compliance assessment monitoring (67%);
- Risk Management (66%);
- Fraud prevention / detection (64%);
- Corporate Governance (51%);
- IT management assessment (45%);

Besides, IAFs are most likely to have a role **in the next 3 years** in the following areas:

- Knowledge management system development (41%);
- Strategic Frameworks (37%);
- Alignment of strategy and performance measurement (36%);
- Benchmarking (35%);
- Corporate Social Responsibility (35%);
- Developing training and education to organization personnel (35%);

Comparing all 21 European countries, we notice (for currently apply and likely to apply in the next 3 years):

- a high involvement of IAFs in the **alignment of strategy and performance measures** in Bulgaria, Estonia, Romania and Spain;
- a high involvement of IAFs in **benchmarking** in Bulgaria, Czech Republic, Romania and Turkey;
- a high involvement of IAFs in **corporate governance** in Netherlands, Romania, Turkey and UK & Ireland;
- a high involvement of IAFs **corporate social responsibility** in Portugal, Romania, Spain and Turkey;
- a high involvement of IAFs in **developing training and education of organization personnel** in Bulgaria, Finland, Norway and Romania;
- a high involvement of IAFs in **disaster recovery** in Estonia, Greece, Romania and Turkey;
- a high involvement of IAFs in **evidential issues** in Bulgaria, Cyprus, Romania and Turkey;
- a high involvement of IAFs in **emerging markets** in Cyprus, Greece, Romania, Turkey;
- a high involvement of IAFs in **environmental sustainability** in Bulgaria, Finland, Greece and Romania;
- a high involvement of IAFs in **executive compensation** in Bulgaria, Estonia, Romania and Spain;
- a high involvement of IAFs in **fraud prevention / detection** in Bulgaria, Cyprus, Norway and Turkey;
- a high involvement of IAFs in **globalization** in Bulgaria, Finland, Greece and Portugal;
- a high involvement of IAFs in **intellectual property and knowledge assessment** in Bulgaria, Estonia, Romania and Turkey;
- a high involvement of IAFs in **IT management assessment** in Bulgaria, Estonia, Sweden and Turkey;
- a high involvement of IAFs in **knowledge management systems development review** in Bulgaria, Estonia, Greece and Romania;
- a high involvement of IAFs in **mergers and acquisitions** in Greece, Romania, Spain and Turkey;

- a high involvement of IAFs in **project management** in Bulgaria, Estonia, Romania and Switzerland;
- a high involvement of IAFs in **providing training to the audit committee** in Greece, Romania, Turkey and UK & Ireland;
- a high involvement of IAFs in **regulatory compliance assessment review** in France, Italy, Switzerland and Turkey;
- a high involvement of IAFs in **risk management** in Cyprus, Czech Republic, Estonia and Sweden;
- a high involvement of IAFs in **strategic frameworks** in Bulgaria, Estonia, Romania and Turkey.

Conclusions

It is clear from the study that internal auditing is a young profession for much of Europe: 57 % of the surveyed internal audit functions have existed for less than 10 years, a figure that is also reflected in the average duration of IIA membership. This characteristic is most apparent in Eastern Europe, where the proportion of young internal audit functions is highest. The growth of corporate governance codes and other regulatory requirements over the last ten years may be one of the drivers that have pushed so many organizations to set up an internal auditing function.

We found that responding internal audit practitioners have very diverse backgrounds in terms of education, professional qualifications and professional experience. This indicates that there is no specific 'unique internal auditor's profile', rather that internal auditors are recruited from a wide pool; in our opinion this benefits the profession as well as their employers. The majority of surveyed internal auditors work in listed and privately owned companies, although a substantial group of 25 % of respondents works for the public sector or governmental organisations. This illustrates the growing importance of internal audit in these sectors, especially in Eastern European countries. Respondents from the financial service industry (including banks and insurance companies) were highly represented.

With respect to the overall corporate governance context, the CBOK study shows some remarkable differences within Europe. Firstly, corporate governance documents (e. g. code of conduct, corporate governance codes, audit committee charters) referred to in this study are more commonly used in Northern and Western European countries. Secondly, there are notable differences between practices in European countries regarding audit/oversight committees. Compared to the rest of Europe, only a small number of Eastern European companies have an audit committee. This could be due to the fact that at the time of the study (2006), none of the corporate governance codes in these countries clearly recommended the set-up of an audit committee. This is a key issue as it can be argued that an effective corporate governance system is fundamental to guarantee the effectiveness of the internal audit function.

Given the importance of audit committees, it was noteworthy that only 36 % of the responding CAEs described their function as being an independent position, reporting to the audit committee. This percentage was higher in Northern and Western European countries; in most Eastern European countries, the internal audit function is often in a managerial position reporting to an executive manager. It was remarkable to see that in a lot of cases, the CAE is still appointed and evaluated by the CEO. To balance this situation, it is fortunate that the audit committee and/or board of directors often have also an impact on these decisions. For those respondents that do have an audit/oversight committee, a very large proportion indicate that they have appropriate access to this committee, with half of the responding CAEs indicating that they have private meetings with the audit/oversight committee.

It was surprising to see that 35 % of the respondents still indicate that their internal audit function does not formally measure their added value. For those who do measure added value, the number of recommendations accepted or implemented and the reliance by external auditors on the internal audit function are the most common measures.

In terms of internal audit staffing, about two thirds of the responding CAEs indicate that they had vacancies at the time of the study. The two most common used methods to make up for staff vacancies were reduction of areas of coverage and co-sourcing. Co-sourcing and outsourcing were also quite popular methods of compensating for missing skill sets. It should be noted that in most cases only a small proportion (less than 10 %) of the activities is outsourced. More than half of the responding CAEs expect the proportion of outsourced/co-sourced activities to remain stable in the upcoming years.

The majority of European respondents believe that compliance with The IIA's *International Standards for the Professional Practice of Internal Auditing* is essential to meet the internal auditors' responsibilities to the organization. Even in countries where the profession is relatively young, they follow the guidance included in the *Standards*. Generally, about 80 % of the respondents indicate that their internal audit function fully or partially complies with the IIA Standards. Nevertheless, for some *Standards* (AS 1300 Quality Assurance and Improvement Program and PS 2600 Management Acceptance of Risks), only one third of the participants state they are fully compliant. Reasons given for not using the Standards seem to be related to organizational attributes. More specifically, it turns out that compliance with The IIA *Standards* is not perceived as adding value by many management/board members and is not supported by them. It is clear that one of the major challenges for CAEs is to convince management and the board of the directors of the usefulness of The IIA's *Standards*. With respect to Quality assessment and improvement programs, about half of the respondents indicate that their organization had such a program at the time of the study or has plans to put such a program in place in the next twelve months. However, the use of The IIA's quality assessment review tools is expected to increase in the upcoming years. It should be noted that most Eastern European internal audit functions, although relatively young, seem to be already on track to meet this requirement.

With respect to internal audit activities, European internal audit functions concentrate their agenda on traditional activities such as operational auditing, internal control testing and systems evaluation and control framework monitoring and development. Despite this, the relative importance of traditional audit activities is expected to decrease in the upcoming years, whereas the relative proportion of consulting/advisory activity is expected to increase. In most Northern and Western European countries, the internal audit agenda has become much broader, involving activities such as (*inter alia*) business viability assessments, information risk assessments, IT department assessments, and security issues. The study also demonstrates that internal auditing will continue to evolve in the future by incorporating new responsibilities and developing a role in more areas. The respondents believe that their emerging roles will be concerned with an involvement in the development of a knowledge management system, the implementation of strategic frameworks and the alignment of strategy and performance management. Given the relative shortage of internal auditors (cf. high percentage of vacancies in most European countries), an interesting question is raised: to what extent internal audit functions will be able to manage these growing roles?

Currently the three most extensively used audit tools are risk based audit planning, electronic work papers and analytical review. There is also expected to be an overall increase in the use of the different audit tools in the upcoming years. These results seem to indicate the importance of using tools that could facilitate a growth of the internal audit function, especially in those contexts where the internal audit resources are quite limited. The most important technical skills for CAEs and audit managers are: understanding the business and risk analyses, whereas data collection and analysis, interviewing and identifying types of controls were seen to be key technical skills for audit staff and supervisors. To ensure a high quality of the audit work and an unbiased and fair evaluation, confidentiality and objectivity are considered as the most important behavioural skills for all professional levels. Leadership was also seen as an important behavioural skill for CAEs. In terms of competences, analytical competences are crucial for audit staff whereas communication competences turn out to be more key for supervisors and managers. CAEs, on their part, have to be able to promote the internal audit function within the organisation. Finally, auditing, internal auditing standards and ethics turn out to be the three most important knowledge areas for internal audit practitioners.

Overall, this research report has shown that the internal audit profession differs significantly within Europe in terms of profile of internal auditors, characteristics of the internal audit function, staffing, compliance to The IIA *Standards* and internal audit activities. Most of these differences amongst countries can be, directly or indirectly, linked to a different maturity of the internal audit profession in each of these areas.

Biographical Note

Marco Allegrini (PhD, CPA) is Professor of Accounting and of Internal Auditing at the University of Pisa (Italy). He is head of the bachelor degree in Management and director of the Msc in Finance and Control at the same university. He is author of several publications (books, articles, etc.) in the area of accounting, financial analysis, international accounting standards, and internal auditing. He is member of the committee "Research and Study" of the Italian Institute of Internal Auditing.

Giuseppe D'Onza (PhD) is Lecturer in Risk Management and Operational auditing at the University of Pisa (Italy). He is director of the Msc in Auditing and Internal Control Systems at the same university. He is author of several publications (books, articles, etc.) in the area of international accounting standards, risk management, internal control and internal auditing. He is member of the committee "Area 231" of the Italian Institute of Internal auditing

Robert Melville (PhD, MIIA) is Senior Lecturer in Corporate Governance, Internal Auditing and Management at Cass Business School Londen (UK). He is director of the Master courses in Management at the same business school. Previously, he worked as systems auditor, EDP auditor and information systems auditor in several companies. He is chartered member of the British Computer Society and fellow of the IIA UK & Ireland.

Leen Paape (PhD, RA, RO, CIA) is Managing Director of NIVRA Nyenrode School of Accountancy & Controlling and Professor of Accounting Information Systems at Business University Nyenrode (Netherlands). Previously, he served as Managing Director for the Postgraduate Program Internal/Operational Auditing at Erasmus University Rotterdam (Netherlands). He has been a partner at Pricewaterhouse-Coopers and Executive Director for Protiviti Independent Risk Consulting.

Gerrit Sarens (PhD, CIA, CCSA) is Professor of Auditing and Management Accounting at the Université Catholique de Louvain (Belgium) and Professor Risk Management and Internal Control at the University of Antwerp (Belgium). He published several articles on the role of internal audit in corporate governance in national and international journals. He is Chief Examiner for the Diploma in Internal Audit Practice of the IIA UK & Ireland.